RIKKI FULTON'S
REVEREND I. M. JOLLY

RIKKI FULTON'S
REVEREND I. M. JOLLY

How I found God,
and why he was hiding from me

Tony Roper

BLACK & WHITE PUBLISHING

First published 2002
by Black & White Publishing Ltd
99 Giles Street, Edinburgh, EH6 6BZ

Reprinted 2002, 2003, 2004

ISBN 1 902927 51 6

British Library Cataloguing in Publication Data:
A catalogue record for this book is available
from the British Library.

Cover photograph by Stephen Kearney
Cover design by Tim Byrne

Printed and bound by Creative Print & Design

Introduction

BY **RIKKI FULTON** OBE

It is a strange fact that the Reverend I. M. Jolly came to the BBC courtesy of Scottish Television. When I was making *Scotch & Wry* – and loving every minute of it – Katie and I were members of New Kilpatrick Church, where there was an excellent minister, Alastair Symington, an outstanding preacher who helped his congregation leave the church with a spring in their step thanks to his uplifting and humorous sermons.

When we saw *Late Call* the difference was unbelievable. Glum looking ministers with dreary, gloomy sermons sent you to bed hoping you wouldn't wake up in the morning. And thus the character of I. M. Jolly was created.

What amazed me was the instant reaction of the viewers. Everyone seemed to identify Jolly with someone they knew. Interestingly, not one member of the clergy ever criticised it to my face, and many said 'I know a chap just like that'.

I became very fond of the cantankerous old so-and-so, and the greatest problem I had was keeping a straight face when the audience howled with laughter. Incidentally, the young minister making his first nervous TV appearance and getting drunk on neat gin was the Rev David Goodchild, not I. M. Jolly as many people think.

When *Scotch and Wry* ended, I. M. Jolly became a character in his own right with his own programme. He gave me a great deal of fun, and I sincerely hope you will enjoy his further adventures in this book, written by my dear friend Tony Roper.

My thanks to all the viewers and readers over the years.

Yours aye

Rikki

Acknowledgements

To Rikki and Kate for the many happy hours
we have shared. And to Isobel for her invaluable
help and encouragement.

Tony Roper

RIKKI FULTON'S
REVEREND I. M. JOLLY

D EAR ME.
What a day I've had.
I'm writing this to myself because I think I may have a wee problem and it looks like I'm the only one who can solve it. It could turn out to be a right scunner because it'll mean me indulging in a bit of self-examination – and I usually fail exams.

Oh dear! I've just caught a glimpse of myself in the mirror. I look like I've just eaten a wasp sandwich. Of course, it's not like me to be down in the dumps. I'm usually far too busy bringing joy to my congregation and trying to lift their spirits up. Sometimes they have too much spirits and then I have to lift their bodies up as well, but that's all part of the job.

So it's not in my nature to contemplate my naval, or indeed any other part of my body. No, wait a minute, I tell a lie. I did once gaze at my naval. It was a Monday, but I decided never to do it again because I found an old bit of toast lodged in it which must have fallen in when I was having breakfast in bed on the Sunday. It took me ages to prise it out and made me late for a christening, if I remember rightly, so I made a mental note never to poke about down there again. But that's the only time I have indulged in self-analysis – until now. My reason is as follows.

The morning started like any other. I awoke to the sound of my dear wife Ephesia's gentle, barely audible snoring – it's barely audible because she sleeps downstairs in a bedroom with double-glazed doors and windows. I slipped into my dressing-gown and baffies – which was no mean feat seeing as I was still in my bed and under the covers – then made my way to the bathroom. I decided on a bath rather than a shower, turned on the bath tap, and selected the towel which was least damp so I could dry myself when I'd finished my ablutions.

As I prepared my face for shaving, I mused on the thought

that *life* was a bit like taking a bath. After being out in the rat race of modern society, we feel the need to be cleansed so that we can renew ourselves or, to put it another way, be *born again*. So we immerse ourselves in water – very similar, I think, to the act of *baptism*. We luxuriate in the warmth of the water and feel good as we rub ourselves with a bar of soap (I always use carbolic because Ephesia got a whole box cheap off of the woman who used to do the stairs, but then she won the Lotto, got blotto and she packed in doing the stairs and we got the cut-price carbolic). But just as we're starting to feel relaxed and satisfied that life is good, the soap slips from our grasp and disappears into the dark, murky water sloshing around us. How dark and murky, of course, depends on the last time we had a scrub up, but anyway, we try to find it by feeling around with our feet. It's not there. We may panic and see if it's lodged itself in one of our body's private places. (If it's carbolic, we'll definitely panic.) Still no sign of it. Where can it be?

As we grope for the soap of hope we realise that comfort and contentment are fragile things that need to be nurtured and protected or they will drift away from us and leave us with uncertainty and despair – not to mention a scum-ring round the bath if you live in a hard water area. Just when we give up hope and decide that the next time we buy the soap of hope, we'll buy the soap of hope on a rope so we won't lose it and be left with only one side of our body clean, with a gasp of relief we find it and, as Robert Burns wrote, 'All's well that ends well'.

It was while I was musing along in this fashion that I heard the mail man drop the mail through the letterbox. I didn't at that time attach any particular significance to this as he does it most mornings and usually leaves – apart from Christmas and New Year, when he invariably rings the bell to wish us good tidings and get a tip, and we have this running gag that I never answer the door and he gives it a good kicking, and calls Ephesia and me a pair of miserable lawyers – or is it barristers?

Och! It's something like that.

Anyway, as I was about to shave I noticed that the blade in my razor needed replacing due to fact that it was clogged up with the strong hair of a virile, manly chin. I knew at once, of course, that Ephesia must have borrowed it. She has a tendency to be . . . what's the word? 'Hirsute', that's it. In fact, she has this angora two-piece suit and the first time I saw her wear it I couldn't help notice that she was more hirsute than her suit.

While I was searching in the waste bucket for the blade I had thrown away a week ago because Ephesia had run out of leg wax, I began to muse on how like life trying to have a shave was, and how I could maybe incorporate this into my sermon on Sunday, thereby bringing some meaning into the dreary, dank, dismal existence that passes for life in my congregation. I think the three of them would appreciate me going to all that trouble, and if not, I think they deserve all they get.

I could start the analogy by pointing out that sometimes, for example, we have 'close shaves'; other times we just 'scrape by' or get all het up and 'into a lather'. I was really starting to enjoy myself when I felt my feet slide out from under me. I landed on the bathroom linoleum – not with a bang, as I expected, but with a splosh, and that's when I realised I had let the bath overflow. Was this also like life? 'Who gives a toss?' was the conclusion I came to as I sat down to bail out the bathroom.

It must have been about an hour later that I heard Ephesia call to say there was a letter for me from the Church of Scotland Synod. As I walked down the stairs, the smell of burnt toast and stewing Typhoo told me that Ephesia was making breakfast. We used to have All Bran and prunes, but the plumbing bills were astronomical so we've settled for toast and tea now.

The letter lay on the table next to the butter dish. I removed it quickly before Ephesia sat down because she is a wee bit absent-minded and could quite easily have buttered the letter and eaten it instead of the toast. Come to think of it, it would probably have tasted better than the toast.

I had no idea why the Synod would want to write to me. Perhaps, I thought, as I opened the envelope with the knife I had just spread jam on my toast with, they wanted my advice on some matters ecclesiastical. Wiping the jam off the letter, I began to read and my jaw must have hit the floor with what I saw in front of me. I quote:

Reverend Jolly

It has come to the attention of the Synod that Church attendances in Scotland have fallen dramatically. We have over the last year had an investigation into why this should be and the reason, after exhaustive questioning of parishioners the length and breadth of the land, is boredom. Apparently, the way that certain ministers carry out their parish duties is now considered old-fashioned and behind-the-times. The youth of today complain that certain ministers are quite simply out of touch.

The Synod decided that the easiest way to weed out these ministers was to send observers to do a head count of attendances at Church on Sundays. The resultant figures did not give us cause for rejoicing. However, even amidst the sea of indifference that we were subjected to, one parish stood out above all others. *Yours*. The observer counted *four* people, then had to do a recount when he discovered he had included himself. The actual count, therefore, was *THREE*.

In view of this fact, we would like you to consider the following suggestions.

It is the opinion of the Synod that the Reverend I. M. Jolly would benefit from having a close look into himself to determine the reasons for the phenomenally low attendances at his church. It is suggested that maybe the practice of writing down his thoughts and actions may give him an insight into the aforementioned lack of interest in his ministry. The observance of the said writings we hope will lead him to a closer understanding of himself, his parishioners, and indeed of his immediate family.

We propose giving the Rev. Jolly one year to boost the congregation substantially or we will have to look favourably on receiving a letter of resignation from him, thereby saving the stipend that a financially-challenged Church of Scotland can ill afford.

Hoping this finds you well.

Wilson Simmons

WILSON SIMMONS
SECRETARY FOR THE CHURCH OF SCOTLAND

* * *

Never having been one to shirk my duty or a challenge I have therefore determined that I will write down, starting from now, all that I feel of import to my effectiveness as a minister and a stipend receiver. I have also determined not to inform Ephesia of the Synod's ultimatum. She would only worry unnecessarily and may also turn violent.

THIS MORNING I AWOKE to face the first day of The Ultimatum. I awoke about seven-thirty having slept like a baby through the night – that is to say, I had messed myself and was sucking my thumb. I realised this was only a form of comfort blanket and not a solution, although I must confess the blanket was anything but comfortable.

As I lay there listening to the birds coughing, I began to feel sorry for myself and even quite depressed – which is, of course, foreign to my normally jovial and upbeat way of thinking. What could I do to save my parishioners from the heartbreak of having to say goodbye to me, and to save me from the heartbreak of having to sign on the dole?

Nothing. That was the answer, do nothing. Well, when I say 'nothing' I of course don't mean that literally. I will have to breathe and eat and so on. I mean do nothing *extra* – nothing that I wouldn't have done before I got that literary equivalent of the Sword of Dampclaes over my head.

Right, time to take stock of the problem. How many people are in my parish? I looked in the church records and I discovered there were 83,109. Of those, 12,206 are Mooslems, or is it Muslems? I'm not sure. I know it's not 'Muslin' because Ephesia has a blouse made out of that. Anyway, whatever the spelling there are definitely 12,206 of them. There are 7,204 Hindus, or is it Hindoos? No, it cannae be 'Hindoos' – that sounds like the last pidgin into the dookit. Then there are fifty-two Bhoodists, six aetheists, and two Wee Frees. That leaves 63,639 Christians to play with (thank God I can spell Christians).

Of those 63,639, there are 28,712 Roaming Catholics. That leaves, by my reckoning, 34,927 Church of Scotland Protestants – of which three come to my church regularly. Oh dear. Still, on the bright side it's one more than the Wee Frees have.

The trick I have to pull off is how to attract those 34,927 Proddies back to the fold. Even for me, with my effervescent personality and bubbling optimism to call on, this is a tall order. I could try the usual bring-and-buy sales, church raffles, Bible discussion classes and so on, but somehow I don't think that, thrilling as those events are, they are what's going to turn the ship around, so to speak.

It seems there is nothing for it but to just be myself and trust in God to bring me through the crucible that the Synod has put in my path. Indeed, had not most of *His* followers had similar trials and tribulations to face? Did not Moses lead the Israelis out of bondage into a land of milk and honey? The Bible tells us that he *did*. Mind you, I'm sure Moses didn't start with just three, but that is the task in front of me and I know that He will not let me down. So as Craig Brown, the erstwhile Scottish football manager, used to say, 'Just play your own game' – that must be my *modi operandus* from now on. I must go about the parish business as usual, spreading light with a cheery word here and a merry quip there and the odd time going down on bended knees and begging the three or four thousand stay-aways to 'gonnae come back, please'.

As I went into church this morning I ran into one of my regulars, old Mrs Maclumpha and her pal Miss McGuffie – or, to give them their full names, Lorna Maclumpha and Peaches McGuffie. Neither of them are particularly, what you would call, attractive – indeed, Ephesia once remarked that somebody must have sat on Lorna's face while it was still warm.

They formed an instant friendship when, on introducing Peaches' husband, Lorna asked her, 'Is this your first husband?'

'No,' replied Peaches, 'my second.'

With a dismissive glance Lorna said, 'Aye! He wouldnae be my first choice either.'

This was enough to cement a lifelong friendship that has endured through thick and thin – or in their case, thick and thick, neither of them having been last down to the dinner table when they were in their formative years.

When Peaches' husband finally passed on, Lorna was a true

friend to her. Indeed, Peaches often tells the story of how, on finding her husband with his head in the oven, it was Lorna who pointed out to him that it was an electric oven and he was going about it all wrong.

'If it hadn't been for her, I might never have known the joys of widowhood,' she says with a smile and a sigh of relief.

After Aeneus (that was his name) finally departed from this earth, again it was Lorna who managed to quell the tears of despair coming from Peaches' very soul and turn them into tears of joy when, after rummaging around in the kitchen drawers, she exclaimed with a cry of exaltation, 'It's alright, I've found his insurance policies!'

Now, although as I've said, Mrs Maclumpha was a regular attendee, her friend and ally Peaches was not, so it was more than a little surprising to find them both sitting in a pew side by side. My heart skipped a beat. This was maybe my chance to swell the congregation up to four.

Putting on my best cheery smile I said, 'And to what do we owe the honour of seeing you two lovely ladies sitting in the pew this morning?'

With a look that made my spine stiffen Lorna growled, 'You owe the honour to the fact that some idiot varnished the pews and never put a sign up. It wouldn't have been you, would it?' she said accusingly.

You know, sometimes it's better to tell a white lie if it's going to save a person a lot of trouble and grief. This was one of those times, I felt, and I was one of those persons.

'Eh! No! Not guilty this time,' I white-lied. 'It must have been the . . . the . . . eh! . . . the . . . the . . . pew painter. Yes, that's who it's been. How long have you been here?'

'All night!' said Peaches, giving me a malevolent stare. 'We both came in to rest our feet, sat doon and we've been stuck here all night. We're absolutely freezing.'

My mischievous sense of humour let me down when, before

I could stop myself, I quipped, 'Well let's hope you haven't caught pew-monia.'

As the handbag whistled past my head, I heard the sound of cloth being rent asunder and the twanging of what I think may have been knicker elastic as both Lorna and Peaches leapt up at me from their previous stationary positions. I think it was as I passed out from the original blow to the temple – or it may have been the kick in my groin – that I decided not to risk asking Peaches if she would like to fill out a church membership form. Indeed, as I slipped into unconsciousness, I mused on the fact that rather than increasing the congregation to four I had, in fact, reduced it to two.

My last thought as I passed out was not a happy one. I was now neck and neck with the Wee Frees.

AS IF IT ISN'T ENOUGH to have The Ultimatum hanging over my head, my idyllic home life has taken a turn for the worse. I really don't know what is happening to my world. I am confused, perplexed and dumbfoonert. The reason? Let me set it down and see if I can make sense of this shock to my system that has driven all my worries about falling church attendances and impending unemployment on to the back boiler.

Something has happened that I would have thought impossible, beyond the realms of the imagination of even Jakey Rowling, who wrote the definitive account of Pansy Potter. It appears that Ephesia has *a fancy man*.

I'll say it again, *a fancy man*.

I can't believe it. What man would fancy Ephesia? I married her, but even I never *fancied* her.

As these writings are private, I can reveal that Ephesia and I had to get married. Her mother said, '*Over my dead body*', and it just seemed too good an opportunity to miss.

The look of bewilderment on Ephesia's face was best described as astonishment when she realised that, despite all the odds – i.e. no money, no personality, no dress sense, no *common* sense – she had actually *landed a man*. I can still remember proposing, and her eyes filling up with tears when she nodded her acceptance with the words, 'Well, any port in a storm, I suppose.'

I must set down the reasons why I believe she's having an *affray de coeur*. This morning while I was spying on – eh, I mean, happened to be glancing into the living-room of the stunning blonde who has just moved into the house across the road – merely, of course, to find out if there was any way I could bring a little joy into the undoubted shock and trauma we all experience when we are involved in a flitting. As I watched with fascination I know I was certainly traumatised. She had long, golden, shiny hair that fell gently over her pert and perfectly proportioned bosoms, which were barely constrained in what I would hazard a guess was a 38D cup, black silk bra and a matching black silk underskirt which barely concealed the tiny thong underneath clinging to . . .

What was it I wanted to write about again? Oh aye! Ephesia's fancy man. Well, I was trying to think of a way to, eh! . . . help the new neighbour settle in when I heard Ephesia's voice quivering through the air from the upstairs bedroom.

'Yes! Yes!' she bellowed seductively, 'I can't wait until tomorrow when I'll be holding your hand and the electricity between us will make our spirits soar into the air. Till then, my sweet.'

My sweet? Unless she was talking to the sofa and two chairs, she was on the phone to a fancy man and I meant to find out who. I felt betrayed, sullied, and it seemed to me that our marriage vows had been turned into a mockery. Such was my depth of anguish that I dropped the binoculars on the floor.

It is, of course, at moments like this that my calling as a minister can help me through the darkness of uncertainty by recalling a quotation from the Good Book that will help soothe the troubled mind. Almost at once I recalled the words of another man who centuries ago had written, 'And there came from the East a man who was sick of the palsy, and he said, "See this palsy – *I'm sick o' it!*"', or words to that effect. I must try to appear calm and in control of myself so she doesn't suspect that I know she has taken my heart and used it as a mere plaything. Before I do that, however, I'll just have another wee keek out the window and see how the new neighbour's settling in.

I LEFT OFF YESTERDAY by telling you the dreadful dilemma I was in on overhearing Ephesia phoning her fancy man while I was eyeballing the new neighbour. I determined to follow her and see for myself what kind of warped, home-breaking, irrational nutter would actually find her attractive. The outcome of this odyssey was to prove even weirder than I could ever have dreamed, and I've had some pretty weird dreams – like the one where I'm trapped bollock-naked in an assembly line for a factory that manufactures false buttocks, armed with only a fish slice and a post-war army gas-mask. How's that for weird, eh? Sorry, I digress.

Deciding on the best way to catch the pair of them at it, I followed her when she left the house, adopting the rather cunning disguise of a High Church of England choirboy. The ruse worked very well, except for the odd scoutmaster, priest with an American accent, lifeboy's captain and high court judge, who all very kindly wanted to take me home for a cup of tea. Actually, I never realised we had such a surfeit of high court judges walking about the streets. You learn something new every day in life, don't you?

I traced the wanton hussy formerly known as the wife to a close mouth in Sighthill where I observed her entering the first-floor flat on the left. I wanted to catch them at it so I decided to give them a bit of time to get into . . . well, God alone knew what they were up to, never mind into. I whiled away the time talking to a nice chief constable, who also wanted to take me to his place for a cup of tea. I must say, having to deal with all the nasty and sordid side of life in my calling it did my heart good to see that there were so many of our civic leaders willing to stretch out the hand of friendship to lonely choristers. I suppose if you are a chorister, it makes it all worthwhile, singing in a high-pitched voice while waiting for your testicles to drop, knowing that the high heid yins are behind you with a helping hand.

The chief constable left when his bag of sweets was finished and I thought, *now's* the time to expose her and have a decko at the matinee idol. Carefully placing my ear to the letterbox, my senses were sent even further on the road to disbelief. Try as I might, I could not deny that I heard the sounds of loud moaning coming from inside this carnal house. Even more shocks awaited my tormented soul when I realised that there were more than two voices to be heard. My God, I thought, it's an orgy.

I heard a voice shout, *'Hold my hand.'*

'Don't let go,' said another.

'Oh yes! Yes! Hold on tight! Tighter! Tighter! The eight of us must do it together.'

My senses took another body-blow. *Eight*? There were more at her orgy than I had as a congregation.

The moaning intensified and grew to a crescendo and then just . . . stopped.

I heard a male voice say, 'Has everyone had enough?'

'Oh aye,' responded a woman, 'I couldnae handle another session like that.'

'Me neither,' chorused the rest of the fornicators.

Another male voice issued the command, 'Somebody put the light oan.'

Then my heart froze. I could hear Ephesia's unmistakable voice huskily say, 'That was the best yet, eh?'

I could stand no more. I kicked open the door and, cassock flying, flew like an avenging angel into the veritable cauldron of evil, the chamber of wantonness, the cesspool of sex that was very much like somebody's kitchen. In point of fact, it *was* somebody's kitchen; it had a table in the middle, round which were eight people fully dressed, one of which was a wee woman wi' what looked like porridge coming out her mouth.

'Who the hell are you?' she spluttered. 'I've goat a moothful o' ectoplasm here and it's highly dangerous to interrupt a

medium when she's swallyin' porridge . . . I mean, ectoplasm that can sometimes be mistaken for porridge.'

A small man with a cardigan boasting a hole in each elbow rushed to the woman's side. 'Are you alright, Madam Mazweet?' he said anxiously, wiping the porridge from her second chin.

Then a large brute of a man with a trumpet hidden up one of his sleeves grabbed me by the throat and hissed, 'Who do you think you are, interruptin' the Sighthill Society of Spiritualists' Sunday night seance?'

Ephesia drew me one of her looks, the type of look that married men the world over understand without a word being spoken between them and their other halves. It's a look that simply says, *Shut it. I'm not with you.*

With all their eyes turned to me waiting for an explanation, I could only reply, '. . . Eh! Was it not you that phoned aboot the exorcism then?'

AS THEATRE CHAPLAIN I'm strangely never asked to attend the opening nights of the various offerings that are fed to us masquerading under the name of entertainment. However, I was so needing taken out of myself that I went to the theatre this evening to see the local amateur production of *The Mousetrap* by John Reginald Christie. It was very enjoyable and I flatter myself that I may have even added to the enjoyment of the audience because I had actually seen it before. So in my opening curtain speech I told them all who done it, which saved them the bother of trying to figure it out for themselves. In fact, the director of the play was so pleased I could hear him shout out from the wings backstage, 'Oh, well done. Well bloody done', and the audience chorused in agreement with him, which pleased me, except for the fact that they all got my name wrong. They seemed to think it was 'Pratt' – indeed, some of them thought it was 'Plonker'.

Despite their shows being for the most part a pile of dog's poo, I'm very fond of the theatre and indeed the theriatricals who work in it. Well, maybe 'work' isn't the right word – 'fart about' is probably more accurate (excuse the French). (Is 'fart' a French word?)

The first time I ever served as a theatre chaplain was very memorable for me due chiefly to the fact that I was not aware that they were actually performing a play when, wandering around backstage, I innocently walked through a door and found myself in Ancient Rome where men in skirts were stabbing a man in a long dress with rubber daggers.

I heard someone shout out what sounded like, 'Et tu Brutey'. I thought they said, 'Zat you, Brutey?' So I said, 'No, it's the meenister.' The audience all started laughing and applauding and shouting, '*More! More!*' so I did it again, and they positively howled. I think this was memorable for me because it was the first time I discovered I had this gift of being able to cheer folk up and lift them out of the hurly burly of their tedious, dreary,

flat and humdrum existences.

Mind you, even I can't seem to please everyone because even as the audience were shouting their appreciation of my contribution, the actors in the skirts decided to leave the man in the long dress and, turning their attention on me, proceeded to try to strangle me and punch me on the nose. They obviously had had *their* noses put out of joint so they wanted to put mine out as well.

The theatre management seemed delighted with my contribution. Indeed, they were so appreciative that they invited me to be in their pantomime – at least, I think that's what they meant. The actual words they said were, 'It'll be a cold winter before we let you back in here.'

So that was nice of them.

I HAVE WRACKED MY BRAIN constantly and asked for divine guidance at least three times a day – i.e. morning, noon and night – for a solution to the Church's missing members problem, with no immediate sign of success. I've decided still to keep Ephesia in the dark as to the Synod's ultimatum, or it might not only be the Church that is missing a member or two.

She's been asking when I'm due my annual two weeks' leave. I must admit there are times when I sit alone with my secret burden, I feel that maybe a holiday would help recharge the batteries and give me the inspiration to solve this dilemma. My parishioners are so concerned about my workload. The two of them seem to be urging me to go on an activity break; there's never a day goes by but one of them will remark, 'Is it no' aboot time you and her took a hike?'

Indeed, we did go on a trekking holiday many years ago. It was wonderful. We were in the first flush. It was my first parish and the manse had an inside toilet. However, you get bored with only pulling the plug for relaxation so we decided to go on a trekking holiday. In fact, if I remember rightly that was at the behest of the verger that time, who shouted at us, 'Why don't you two take a walk? . . . A long, long walk.'

So early one morning we set off with a song in our hearts and a spring in our steps. It was a typical Scottish summer's day. Our eyes stung with the pain as the rain lashed down and the wind whipped past us. Truth to tell, we were all for turning back but our wonderful parishioners spurred us on by singing the words of that grand old song, 'Will Ye No' Come Back Again?' Except that in their excitement, they got mixed up and sang, 'You'll No' Come Back Again, Will Ye?' So, with a cheery wave and soaking feet we started out to sample the wild beauty of our native land.

I can still remember that first day as if it were yesterday, singing hymns, quoting from the Good Book, Ephesia's hair blowing in the wind, both of us too tired to run after it, straining under the weight of the two backpacks (eventually I carried one of them).

We came to the top of an extremely high hill and as we'd been at it all day we thought we deserved a wee break (well, you do when you've been at it all day, don't you). So, we sat down. And as we sat there the sun started to nod his head and bid us adieu as he sunk into the vale of twilight that painted itself on to the delicate beauty of the valley, which lay in quiet supplication before us. But the most magical moment was when we saw a stag about fifty feet downwind of us, standing taut and proud, his magnificent antlers glowing golden in the setting sun, and it was at this moment of sublime solitude that Ephesia turned to me in the stillness and broke wind. Neither of us said a word; we didn't need to. Mind you, the stag's back legs buckled a bit with the impact.

We've been on many a holiday since, but none of them has ever captured the essence of our relationship the way that one did. The following year we went cycling, after the parish had told us, 'On yer bikes, the pair of you'. Mind you, there was a hint of magic there too, because by the time we came back the entire parish had mysteriously converted to Orthodox Judaism.

Last year was quite unusual in the fact that when I announced from the pulpit Ephesia and I would not be going away at all, the admittedly even then dwindling congregation seemed to want *us* to pay for *their* holidays. They all shouted, '*Give us a break, will ye?*' Oh well, cocoa time.

W HAT A WEEK I've had, ghastly. It started off with me going to prison. Not that I had done anything wrong – the Church of Scotland Synod hasn't quite threatened me with loss of freedom for low attendances just yet. I went to the prison in my capacity as prison chaplain. Strictly speaking, I didn't actually go in my capacity; I went in my *car*.

I'm afraid I'm not quite joined up . . . That's not right either. What is the phrase the young people use? *'Together'*, that's the word. I'm not quite together, but honestly no wonder I'm puggled.

It all started out quite normal. I arrived at the prison entrance and the guards all went through the usual charade of pretending they weren't delighted to see me, such as holding up placards saying, 'PISS OFF YA DICK' (I don't know why people keep getting my name wrong), staging mock demonstrations with *actual* union delegates, and representatives from the prisoners threatening strike action unless I promised not to come within a five-mile radius of the prison – they really do play the joke right up to the hilt.

Anyway, eventually after four hours of this wonderful banter the prison governors sorted it all out by pretending to pay the guards double-time and letting the prisoners have six months docked off from their sentences. The inmates were then assembled in the – eh! what would you call it? – assembly hall, I suppose, and asked if any of them would like to unburden their guilt feelings by spending a couple of hours alone with me. They had a meeting and then they informed me through an official letter that they would rather be locked up with *Al Kaeda*. I must admit that I was a bit hurt because I felt that, over the years, I had built up a relationship with the prisoners, and now this Mr Kaeda had seemingly replaced me in their affections. They even knew his first name was Al, whereas they thought mine was Dick.

In fact, I was so depressed that as I trudged out the assembly room I forgot to lock the door and the next thing I knew the prisoners were all running out the hall, had captured a guard, and were saying they would lock him up alone with me until another substantial lump was knocked off their porridge. I could certainly sympathise with them; after all, there's nothing worse than lumpy porridge.

That night I sat in my own private cell that the prisoners had kindly given to me (it's the nearest you can get to a place of quiet and solitude in prison – in fact, it's called Solitary). The guard who was supposed to share it with me had kindly given the prisoners money to let me have the place to myself. I sat there wondering if Al Kaeda had been given the luxury of a private room, and to my shame I must admit that a small part of me hoped he hadn't. I knew just how exclusive my private room was when I noticed scratched on the wall was the message 'Kilroy was here'. I have to say, I did not expect acts of vandalism from him, even though he has his own show on the telly.

They really do encourage the prisoners to express themselves. Art competitions were obviously very popular because the one who said he had drawn the short straw had been selected to bring me my dinner (thankfully not porridge). I had to smile when he pretended to be bored with my stories from the Old Testament. But I knew I had touched a chord when he shouted to the Lord, 'For God's sake give me peace.'

I realised he knew he was a step nearer Heaven when one of his chums who had come to let him out of my room asked him, 'How was it?' I heard him say, 'Purgatory – that was Purgatory.' My delight was complete when I was told by another art winner that the entire board of governors who had negotiated that I be allowed into the prison were to be rewarded with what is called a golden handshake, but only if they would resign. I'm sure the inmate had got it wrong. What I presume he meant was that they were to be rewarded only if they were to re-sign.

Three days later I found out through what the inmates call the grapevine that the governors had indeed agreed to re-sign – a further six months were to be docked off the prisoners' sentences and the porridge would presumably be lump-free.

As I left the prison gates a strange phenomenon occurred; the prison governors were now getting my name wrong but the inmates were all singing, 'For he's a *Jolly* good fellow!' It seems that Al Kaeda is now *persona non gracias* while yours truly is *persona muchos gracias*.

He does indeed work in mysterious ways.

THE REV. I. M. JOLLY

ISN'T IT WEIRD how your mind can sometimes wander? Just the other day while I was performing a christening for a batch of potential new church members – part of the old hatched, matched and dispatched side of my business) – I was dunking the child in the font when I thought to myself that it was strange that Ephesia and I had never been blessed with progeny. I remember we went to our doctor and we discovered it was my fault. I just thought she was hakkit.

It didn't start off that way, of course. The first night of our honeymoon was quite remarkable. I, of course, had never known a woman before – well, I knew my mother and the woman who owned the dairy, but in a biblical sense I was still without experience of the opposite . . . thingmy's. But that first night was really extraordinary. Almost from the first tentative touch I thought, 'Aye, aye! She's up for it.' I lay there in a quandary, not quite knowing how I should proceed because usually I had been bombed out long before I got to this stage. I could hear her gasping and moaning, squealing and panting. I thought to myself, 'You're away here' . . . Then I found out she had asthma.

She's still quite bad with it – in fact, the other night she was wheezing away to herself as we sat in the living-room watching a roll of wallpaper that was trying to get away from the damp patch behind it. We sat there fascinated as it almost imperceptibly uncurled a hundredth of an inch every half-hour. (It was either that or watch Ainsley Harriet having his house made over by the *Changing Rooms* gang.) Anyway, it was during this interlude that one of those sex pests phoned. I heard the deep breathing, but I was wrapped up in the adventures of our wallpaper so I passed it on to Ephesia who was still rasping away. After ten minutes the pest said to her, 'Did I phone you or did you phone me?'

It's a great pity that we are without offspring. I tried to imagine what the child would be like if it had inherited Ephesia's looks and my disposition. I couldn't, of course. I was still trying to picture in my mind's eye what the wee one would turn out like when I was aware that someone was shouting at me and my person was being shaken and manhandled in a most rough and uncouth way.

'Watch what you're doing,' I shouted.

'Naw! You watch what you're doing,' came a voice out of the air. 'You're droonin' the wain.'

'Och, so I am,' I admitted with a wry smile and a shake of the head. Indeed, I'd got so wrapped up in my meanderings down memory lane that when I dunked the child in, I forgot all about taking it out – a mistake anybody could make, I thought.

Now it was turning a bit blue, I admit, and OK it had stopped breathing. But there was absolutely no need to overreact the way the parents, godparents, grandparents (both sets) and sundry neighbours did. They called me for everything. I tried to calm them all down by smiling and giving them a cheery wave. Unfortunately, while I was attempting this manoeuvre, I dropped the baby into the font, but fortunately that started it breathing again. On the other hand, it was now soaking wet.

I was attempting to make good my wee mistake by wringing it out when the mother fainted and the father tried to nut me. I threw up my hands to defend myself – completely forgetting, of course, I was still with child, so to speak, and hit the father with his own baby.

His reaction was typical, of course, blaming me for the entire episode and offering to help me achieve an internal inspection of my sit-upon by shoving my head up the said sit-upon. As I began what the military call a strategic withdrawal (though probably this was more of a strategic run-like-hell), I could hear him shouting that he would get even with me somehow.

So I've given up on them as potential new church members – for now anyway.

I N TIMES OF DARKNESS, when I feel Despair rest her cold, clammy hand on the back of my neck, and Anguish sends a shiver of distress through my body that makes my flesh creep and goose-bumps appear as my blood starts to run cold and turn to ice in my veins, I always turn to the Good Book for guidance, in order to avoid a nasty chill developing.

This afternoon I was sniffling, my eyes were watery and I was blowing my nose constantly. This, of course, is normal for me but I decided to have a wee read at the Old Testament anyway, just to cheer myself up.

GENESIS 5 VERSE 4

And the days of Adam after he had begotten Seth were eight hundred years and he begat sons and daughters.

CHAPTER 5 VERSE 5

And all the days that Adam lived were nine hundred and thirty years; and he died.

Astonishing, eh! And I mean, that was without a health service. Nine hundred and thirty years? He must have had some pension scheme. Only joking, of course . . . or am I? That is to say, am I only joking that I'm only joking? Who knows? That's the trouble when you're a wag like me, even I myself don't know.

I've often thought of the Bible as God's diary. And the countryside with the beasts of the field providing milk and honey as God's dairy, and the wind that blows the dust from the land and the rain that washes the land as God's daily. But then, that's just me.

Sometimes I gaze up at the firmament, and I see the moon and the millions upon millions of stars that contain countless galaxies that probably contain millions and millions of other galaxies, that again contain millions upon millions of stars, and I think . . . what's the point of sitting here looking at the millions upon millions of stars that contain the millions upon millions of galaxies when I could be in the living-room watching the telly.

So I go into the living-room, switch the goggle box on, and there's Carol Smillie, or Cilla Black or Ainsley Harriet. After about five minutes I switch it off and go outside and watch the moon and the millions upon million of stars that contain countless galaxies that contain millions upon millions of stars that probably contain countless galaxies with millions upon millions of stars, and I think, maybe there's something else on the telly. I go back into the living-room, switch the goggle box on and it's Dale Winton, who is a guest with Cilla Black on Ainsley Harriets' show, and they're frying sausages. *That's entertainment?* Then I think to myself, I wish I had a gun and I'd shoot them all.

Honestly, Ephesia and I sat tuned into this programme where Carol and 'the gang' were giving somebody's house a makeover and I realised I was actually *watching paint dry*. I'll bet you Adam wouldn't have hung about for nine hundred and thirty years if he'd had the telly.

I T'S BEEN A STINKER of a day. Ephesia's in the huff because she's failed her driving test again. Apparently, the examiner asked her to let the clutch out, so she opened the door.

She's gone to a driving school because I refused to teach her any longer on the grounds it was against my religion. Premeditated suicide is not allowed in the Church of Scotland. I remember trying to teach her the rudimentaries, such as checking the vehicle was roadworthy before you set off on your journey.

I said, 'Headlights working?'

She said, 'Yes.'

I said, 'Sidelights working?'

She said, 'Yes.'

I said, 'Left indicator working?'

She said, 'Yes . . . No . . . Yes . . . No . . . Yes . . . No.'

Another time we were on the road and she'd been following behind a lorry for about two or three miles, continually flashing her headlights at the driver and sounding her horn. Finally she turned to me and said, 'At the next set of lights you'll need to get out and tell that lorry driver that he's shedding his load.' It was a gritting lorry. Honest to God, sometimes I think I'll take her to the dentist and have a wisdom tooth put in.

To be honest, this has not been one of my better days, not that I've had that many good ones since the Synod's threat of evicting me. I had toyed with the idea of getting Tommy Sheridan to take up my case, with maybe a few private meetings to avoid the glare of publicity, but the thought of all those hours lying on a sun bed put me off.

Ephesia had a go at me this morning for not taking enough notice of her. Apparently, it's part of the marriage contract that I'm supposed to ignore the fact she's got a face like a bag of chisels, skin like a welder's mitt and hair like a burst Brillo pad and tell her she's dead attractive. I find it hard to lie blatantly, and consequently began to feel the tension that goes with the territory of being married to Ephesia well up inside me.

I knew I was becoming increasingly fretful when I found that I couldn't tie my shoelaces. This was due to the fact that I had absent-mindedly put my shoes on my hands instead of my feet. This is always a giveaway with me, that and putting my trousers on back-to-front then complaining there's a draught coming from somewhere.

So, for relaxation I did what I always do in times of stress; I went to have a wee nosey round a graveyard. I find that the sound of leaves rustling as a soft breeze disturbs their rest, and the atmosphere of quiet serenity makes me feel good about life – that, and the knowledge that they're all dead and I'm not, usually bucks me up no end. Also, the epitaphs are quite often a clue to the person at rest beneath them. I'll never forget the simple message from the family of Alek Pease:

> Under this sod
> And under these trees
> Lies the body of Alek Pease.
> He is not in this hole
> He's gone from his pod
> Cause he's shelled out his soul
> Now he's gone to meet God.

I felt I could identify with Alek Pease because a' like peas as well.

A smile began to play around the edges of my mouth due to my clever play on words as I meandered from stone to stone; there was another that caught my eye.

> Beneath the stone of this epigraph
> There lies a man who liked to laugh
> He laughed at me
> He laughed at you

But I'll bet you a tenner
He's no' laughin' noo.

Ah! The miracle of the human spirit to find humour in even the worst of circumstances. I began to feel the weight of my own problems lift from my shoulders, a spring came back into my step and I started to hum. And then the joy of being alive took me over and I burst into song: 'There Is a Happy Land Far Far Away'. All my cares seemed to float up into the air, there to be picked up by the birds that flew overhead and taken high up into the blue sky to be lost forever. My voice grew louder, and I must say I sang with a gusto that I'd not felt for many a day.

I actually began to do a little jig as I burst into the second verse: 'Ohhh! There is a happy land far far away. . .' I was so caught up with the moment that I failed to notice I was passing a funeral party, burying some loved one no doubt. I was brought back to reality when I heard one of the mourners shout, 'Bloody pervert. You should be ashamed to call yourself a minister.' Another mourner chipped in with, 'That's that maniac Jolly. I'm going to write to your superiors and tell them what you're up to.' The rest then joined in with shouts of, 'Us as well', and 'We're witnesses, so we are.' The only saving grace was that none of the sods of earth they were throwing at me managed to find their target. That and the lucky fact that none of the mourners were members of my congregation, so my flock still stayed at two. A small consolation, but one that I grasped at nonetheless.

There was, of course, no use trying to explain to them what had led to my outburst so I would just have to live with it – which was more than the dearly departed of the funeral party could boast.

I've never understood why the term 'party' is used in the phrase 'funeral party'. I mean, even if nobody liked the corpse, you still wouldn't invite the mourners to a *party*. However, with the price of funerals these days, the phrase '*dearly* departed' is, I would agree, very accurate. The cost of a funeral is way over the top. Why does a cremation cost nearly as much as a burial? At a burial you have to pay for the plot of land to contain the coffin or eventually coffins – and we all know that land is not cheap these days – then you have to pay for the grave diggers to dig the six feet long and twelve feet under. Compare that with the price of a box of matches and you'll begin to see where I'm coming from.

Hastily leaving the graveyard, I wandered around in my angst-ridden state for I don't know how long until finally I decided to give up the ghost and head back to the manse. On the way back home I determined to put a brave face on, and even if it meant bending the truth I would tell Ephesia that she was definitely God's gift, a cut above the average, the sun, moon and stars of my life and anything else she wanted to hear.

Opening the front door, I grasped the bull by the horns (not an altogether inaccurate analogy) and called out, 'I'm home, darling. Where are you?'

'I'm in the living-room, *darling*,' she replied in a voice that was heavy with latent menace.

Gingerly, I prised open the door that led to Heaven knows what – but for the sake of the story we'll call it the living-room – and stood there trying desperately not to have a quaver in my voice when I spoke.

'Had a nice day?' I ventured, tentatively.

She gave me a stare that made my Adam's apple jump up and down involuntarily with the unspoken danger that was almost like a presence in the room.

'I'm waiting,' she intoned with a rasp of astringency that threatened to strip the varnish off the door. I swear that I saw the Swiss cheese plant wilt in the corner of the room where it was cowering behind the ottoman.

'Are you, pet?' I croaked. 'What for?'

Then she spoke the words I was dreading to hear. 'Notice anything different?'

My mind raced. What the hell was it? Think, Jolly, think as if your life depended on it.

'*Well?*' She could sense my fear, and the tone of her voice was as good as a health hazard warning.

I now didn't just think my life depended on my answer, I knew it did. I looked at her intently. What the dickens was it? I could feel her eyes bore into my very soul as she searched for the first sign of indecision that would allow her to let loose. In desperation, I went for a stab in the dark.

'*Oh!* You've had your hair done.'

Our eyes met. She held her gaze. I knew instinctively that my arrow had missed the mark. 'No.'

'Eh! . . . Eh! . . . You've . . . You've . . . You've . . . Eh! . . .'

'What are you trying to say . . . *pet?*' The air was now tingling with a perilous pointlessness that froze the blood in my veins.

'You've had a makeover.' Her head shook from side to side.

'You've had a shave.'

'You've painted the room.'

'That's a new dress?'

'Close, but no coconut yet,' she cackled.

I could tell she was starting to toy with me. My bladder shook and I could feel my bowels start to slacken. Something about the dress. But what?

'It's . . . It's to do with the dress . . . Yes?' My voice was now escaping in gasps.

'That's right. It's to do with the dress. And something else.'

My legs started to buckle and I knew I was lost. I could maybe, just maybe, have had a wild guess about the dress, but now that there was something else to contend with I had to admit defeat.

'I'm sorry,' I burbled, sinking to my knees, 'I don't know. I don't know. Please have mercy.' I had now lost all control and any semblance of manhood was out the window. I even began kissing her feet, and it was then I got a hint of what I had been overlooking. As I was licking and lapping at her feet, I noticed for the first time that she was wearing enormous metal boots with lead soles, and her legs were encased in air-filled waterproof trousers with an array of what looked like oxygen hoses attached. As I sank into a dead faint, I could see Ephesia's face as if through a goldfish bowl.

'That's right, *pet*,' she hissed. 'I'm wearing a deep-sea diver's suit.'

'So near,' I thought, 'so near,' as I sank into inky oblivion.

TRY AS I MIGHT I can not shake loose the sense of foreboding that hangs over my life. What will I do if I can't come up with a solution to my lack of bums on pews?

Last night I found that Murphy O Use would not fold me in his arms and lead me off to dreamland. Sorry, that should be *Morpheus* would not fold me in his arms and lead me off to dreamland. I'm obviously suffering from sleep deporavit . . . depariva . . . lack of sleep. It seemed as if I lay awake half the night grappling with the problem. I even entertained the notion of contacting the leader of the Wee Free community and suggesting that we share congregations, thereby doubling the attendance at a stroke. I abandoned this notion, however, when I realised this would only bring the number at services up to four, hardly enough to satisfy the seemingly insatiable appetite for worshippers that the SS (Sinister Synod) are demanding.

With a sigh and a heavy heart, I swung my legs over the side of the bed and sat upright – or should I say, attempted to sit upright. To my dismay, I found I could not move. Fearing paralysis had taken me in my sleep, I panicked and shouted to my dear wife and sometimes combatant who was sleeping downstairs: 'Ephesia! *Help!* . . . *Help!* I can't move . . . EPHESIA!!!'

But there was no reply – not surprising when I remembered that, as well as her 25-tog-rated duvet-come-nightdress, she always slept with an eye-mask and earplugs. These were encased in a tin World War One home guard's helmet to stop her rolling over and skewering herself with her curlers. Combine that with the four mud facepacks and you'll begin to understand why I really did not harbour much hope from Ephesia's lair, or, as she called it, bedroom.

I also became aware of an excruciating stabbing pain at the bottom of my spine, which I instinctively knew was causing the paralysis that now had me lying powerless on the mattress. As I lay there, helpless and afraid, I admit I started to feel a wee bit sorry for myself. What had I done to deserve this? For all of my adult life, and indeed most of my formative years, I had selflessly served my Church and fellow human beings. But now I was being punished and I knew not what for. To lose the support of the Church of Scotland High Heid Yins was a big enough blow to the old breadbasket, but not to be able to walk again was definitely sticking the knife in. Lifting my eyes to the ceiling, I howled in anguish.

'What have I done to deserve this? Lift this burden from me. Let me rise from this mattress and walk again. Look down on thy servant and . . .' Wait a minute . . . *Mattress*? Of course, I had meant to change the mattress cover last night but was so tired I elected to leave it until this morning.

A slice of spasmodic pain shot through the bottom of my spine. As I turned involuntarily to check that my memory was not playing me false, I tried again to raise myself but found it impossible. Tentatively, I slid my hand around the base that I was lying on and could feel that there was indeed no top sheet. As my hand explored further under my body, it came to my spine which was starting to become numb. The reason for my inertia at once became clear. The cord of my pyjama bottoms had become entwined round a spring that had shot through the mattress, thus holding me fast to the bed. Lifting my eyes to the ceiling once more I explained, 'Sorry. False alarm. I'm alright.' I felt very foolish until I remembered that my father used to say, 'Son! Some days you're the pigeon and some days you're the statue.' For now, I had been awarded statue status, but tomorrow? I could be head bum bombardier.

With that cheery thought, I extricated myself from the offending spring and set my jaw to face the day ahead.

H AVING WASHED and dressed myself, I put on
my spectacles (actually they're Ephesia's spectacles –
she makes me wear them because she wants me to
see things through her eyes) and made myself a cup of tea and
some toast. I heard the paperboy drop the morning rag through
the letterbox. Sliding along the wall, I hid behind the door until
he stopped shouting through the said letterbox for the money
due from last month's delivery.

There was, as usual, nothing but doom, gloom and despair in
the news, so settling down with the eager anticipation of a right
good read I began to forget my own troubles and wallow in
other peoples'. I always turn to the 'Thought for Today' section
as it can often give me inspiration for my sermon. Today's was
quite thought-provoking: 'A great composer can bring tears to
your eyes. But then again, so can a mechanic making up your
garage bill'. I made a mental note to show this to the paperboy.

I was just about to give Ephesia a wake-up knock on the door
when an article caught my eye that made me almost choke on
my tea and toast. It read as follows:

<u>CHURCH OF SCOTLAND MINISTER IN BIG LOTTO WIN</u>

It is understood that a church minister has amassed a
large sum of money as a result of regularly investing
in the Lotto. The identity of the lucky pastor has not
been divulged. However, Lotto sources seemed to be
dropping hints at the winner's name by insisting that
the minister involved was feeling *Jolly*.

They also insisted that the ecstatic ecclesiastic intended
to give most of his millions away to deserving cases in
his parish.

I was livid with anger. This article seemed to be hinting that I was the recipient of this obscene amount of money, which I wasn't. For a start, Ephesia was too tight with my allowance to let me fritter a pound away on Lotto tickets. Even if she had, I would have kept the pound to put into my Battle of Waterloo toy soldiers' fund. I only had a sergeant and two drummer boys, so it would have come in very handy indeed.

Right, this rumour had to be nipped in the bud before it sprouted wings and took off to Heaven knows where. Hastily putting on my coat, I stuck the evil rag in my pocket and set off for the editor's office.

Striding down the street, I was going over in my mind what to say to this idiot when I was hailed from the other side of the street.

'A very good morning to you, Reverend Jolly. And how is your lovely wife?'

I looked up in surprise. 'Are you talking to me?' I asked in amazement, for I had seen this man many times and he had always ignored me.

'Of course, Reverend. The wife and I will see you at church on Sunday I hope?'

'Eh! Yes. OK,' I replied in an admittedly puzzled tone of voice. Still, never one to look a gift horse in the mouth, I gave him a big smile and then started off for the felons of Fleet Street again.

I was wondering if I should maybe try threatening to sue when again I was interrupted by a voice, this time almost at my ear.

'It's lovely to see you, Reverend Jolly,' said this smiling wee woman. 'I wonder if you would book me a place in the front pews for Sunday? I've heard so much about the wonderful sermons you preach.'

I had no idea what she meant, so it was with a note of incontinence in my voice that I asked, 'Have we met?'

She gave my arm an affectionate squeeze. 'Sadly no, but I've always been a huge fan. It's just that I was always a little shy, so I was a bit awe-struck and frightened to say hello to . . .' she smiled coyly, 'the great man himself, or should it be – yourself?'

I stared dumbstruck. '*Eh!* You should just have said,' I replied modestly.

'Really?' she asked with an impish note to her voice.

'Oh aye. There are times when I don't feel all that great. I'll certainly keep you a seat at the front on Sunday, Mrs . . . ?'

'Hegarty. Bridget Hegarty. Do you think you could keep a seat for my husband and our eight of a family as well?'

'Eh! I suppose so.' This was too good to be true. 'What church do you normally go to?'

'St Patrick's,' she informed me.

My mind was starting to go in circles. 'Could I ask, if it's no' too cheeky, are you a Protestant?'

'No. Catholic, but we're willing to change if you would let us join your church.'

Shaking her by the hand I babbled, 'No bother. Come and see me after the service and I'll show you the ropes. Consider yourself one of us.'

I was just about jumping for joy. At last, after all these years, my sermons were beginning to reap the wild harvest. Oh boy! Wait till I tell the Synod about this, I chuckled to myself. Twelve new converts in the one day and ten of them of the Roman persuasion. I could just visualise them grovelling on their knees to me: 'I wonder, Jolly, if you would accept a job as Moderator? Ephesia would, of course, have the title of Moderatoress.'

There and then I decided to forget about the newspaper mistake and hurry home to share the good news with the wife of the future Moderator of the Church of Scotland. Although I had to make sure that I did not blot my copybook by letting her in on the fact that I had not told her about the Synod's ultimatum. That would remain my secret.

What should have been a ten-minute walk took over an hour.

It seemed like every couple of steps there was a new parishioner wanting to join as a full church member.

Throwing the door open with an exuberance I hadn't felt for years, I was about to call out to Ephesia when she flew at me from the kitchen, pinning my arms to my sides in the tried and trusted way she had of rendering me helpless.

'What's this about you having won the Lotto?' she said, her eyes narrowing and her hair raised at the nape of her neck. 'Where did you get the money from?' She was shaking me like a rag doll. If I didn't answer before she got into full attack mode I could be dead in the water. Her ears were already starting to pin back and flatten at the side of her head, always a sign of imminent danger.

'It's a mistake,' I squeaked. 'The newspaper has got it wrong. I have no money hidden anywhere.' She knew I wouldn't dare lie to her. Her grip softened and I slid down the wall. 'How did you find out?' I said breathlessly.

'The phone hasn't stopped ringing for the last hour. Hundreds of well-wishers and parishioners wanting to congratulate you, asking for forms to become reinstated as members and then asking what were the conditions required to qualify as a deserving case.'

'Isn't it wonderful,' I enthused. 'My flock has seen the light and are returning in droves to the fold. This is the culmination of my years in the wilderness. Finally they have gleaned what my ministry is about.'

'I'll tell you what they've gleaned,' said the unofficial Moderatoress. 'They've gleaned that you might be stinking rich and they're trying to get their grubby hands on some of it.'

I tried to disguise the look of pity in my eyes as I searched her face for some glimmer of humanity. I need hardly add I searched in vain.

S UNDAY HAS ARRIVED and I'm quivering with excitement. There is a tingle in the air that is almost a hymn to happiness. I said as much to one of the new church officers.

'That'll be right,' he agreed.

Peeking out through a crack in the doorframe I saw, for the first time that I can ever recall, standing-room only in my church. Even the newspaper that reported the Lotto story had turned up, no doubt to report on the good news that religion was back on the agenda, thanks to yours truly.

Ephesia still persisted in the notion that this resurgence was due to the inherent greed in people who thought I was loaded and was about to dole out handfuls of cash. I couldn't wait to see her face when she was proved wrong. I'd never actually seen her proved wrong so you can appreciate my imminent sense of triumph.

I was also congratulating myself on not succumbing to the temptation of inviting the soon-to-be-highly-embarrassed Church of Scotland Synod to witness the new phenomenon that was the Reverend I. M. Jolly. Let them read about it in the national press, was my thinking.

I had decided my sermon was going to be on the return of the prodigal son (a little dig at the Synod), but first I would get the false Lotto story out of the way so the flock could concentrate on my message. There was no room for any more worshippers, so why delay their hunger for me any longer.

I swept through the door and up to the pulpit – the roar of applause like music to my ears – then, unbelievably, they burst spontaneously into:

You are our sunshine, our heavenly sunshine,
You make us happy, when skies are grey,
You'll never know, how much we love you,
Please don't take our sunshine away.

A man stood up at the back of the hall and shouted, '*One*

46

more time!' Try as I might, I could not get them to stop singing. A tear of – let's face it – relief escaped from a corner of my eye as the audience (I mean, *congregation*) started to settle down.

Surveying them with what I can only describe as quiet confidence, I started my sermon.

'First of all, let me give you the good news. I have not won the Lotto,' I said with a smile on my face, which was immediately wiped off by the sound of people leaving in droves.

As I stood there, listening to the sound of squealing from people being trampled underfoot in their haste to get out, I thought,

'Oh well! Easy come. Easy go.'

M Y PREVIOUS WORRIES of the Synod's warnings are as nothing compared to my present predicament. I am writing this from under the kitchen table. The reason for this unusual location is not to do with me trying to retrieve a piece of bread – or, indeed, any kind of food that may have dropped under the table. I am, in truth, *hiding*. Hiding from Ephesia.

You see, it's springtime, and whereas I used to hide from her at this time of the year because her hormones would kick in and she would come after me demanding her conjugial rights (to this day I still shudder when I recall how I would be hiding in a cupboard, not daring to breathe as I heard her sniffing the air for the scent of fear that would give me away) now the breeding hormone has been replaced by the cleaning hormone, and the mating cry has changed from, 'Let's do something filthy dirty. I need rutting', to, 'This place is filthy dirty, it needs gutting'.

She's upstairs now in a cleaning frenzy. I'm desperate to go to the toilet but I can't because she's nailed up the door. Before that she was in there, hoovering the toilet roll after tying one end to our wee dog's tail and chasing him round the house to unravel it. She's at present scrubbing the dog's bottom with a wire scrubbing brush, and I'm under this table because *I'm* next.

The woman is possessed. If it can't move out of her road, she washes it, scrubs it, dusts it, has another look then screams, '*You're still filthy!*' and attacks it again. Last year the postman made the mistake of delivering a parcel by hand. '*Look at your nails,*' she howled and, before he could retreat, he was stripped and in the bath along with a sackful of letters being sponged down while lying in lily-of-the-valley toilet water. As if that wasn't bad enough, after she'd towel-dried him *and* his letters, she then gave him a coat of white gloss paint 'to freshen him up'. The paperboy was a nervous wreck, and it took the fire brigade a whole day to coax the milkman's horse down off the roof of the coal shed.

Oh no! An ominous silence has descended on the house. This can only mean she has remembered that I am somewhere *in* the house and that I have not been cleansed, ethnically or otherwise. This will require all of my native cunning, not to mention divine interception, if I am to escape the wire brush syndrome . . .

I can smell antiseptic, Dettol and Vim scouring powder. This means she is perilously close, so I'll have to stop for a moment as the scratching of my pen will be picked up by her radar. My heart beat feels like a timpanist is practising the *1812 Overture* on my chest . . .

An hour and a half has passed. I think she's gone. I'll just lift up the table cloth and risk a look . . . I can't see her abou*aghhhhhhhhhhhhhhhhhhhhhhhhhhh*.

EVEN MY CHEERFUL and normally light-hearted disposition has been overcast today as I have been saddled with a visit from my brother Ranald – or, to give him his full name, Ranald Urquhart. He was named after my father, which made him Ranald Urquhart Jolly the Second, a decision which was possibly not fully thought through, because as I was named I. M. Jolly, this unfortunately made him R. U. Jolly 2? And I have to say, the answer was usually no.

He is my younger brother and of course must have been heavily influenced by me. He even wanted to follow me into the clergy, but when I took him for an interview they rejected him on the grounds of, and I quote, 'But that would be two of you.'

He took the rejection quite badly and I think may even have over-reacted slightly when, on taking his leave of the selection committee, he invoked, if I remember rightly: *'Lucifer and the hordes of Hell. The beast of Hades and the sons of Satan to kick your sanctimonious airces until they bleed.'*

Ranald tried various other occupations that might have suited his – for want of a better word – personality, but not with any great success. He had always nursed a secret ambition to work in an undertaker's and eventually managed to dig himself up a job as chief coffin carrier with a local funeral director. We all thought he was doing quite well at the undertaking, but they had to redeploy him because they said he had an attitude problem due to the fact that, as he was carrying the coffin from the church, he kept smiling at the grieving family members and referring to the deceased as, 'That lucky bastard'. So they transferred him to a less-damaging-to-customer-care side of the business, and gave him the post of grave-digger.

With the grave-digging we thought he had truly found his niche. But again he blew it by throwing himself into the grave just before the coffin was lowered in and shouting at the recently deceased as he was being lowered into his final resting place,

'Bugger off, I was here first.'

He can, however, be extremely charming on occasion and as we sat down to dinner he asked me with a shy smile if I would allow him to say Grace.

'That would be very nice,' I enthused, ignoring Ephesia's warning glance.

He folded his hands and bowed his head, then when we had done likewise, he said Grace:

'As I sit doon this meal to eat,

I have no thought of leavin',

But I'm willin' to bet, after I've ett,

My stomach will be heavin'.

Amen.'

Ephesia laughed the whole thing off, of course, and jokingly broke his nose with one of her size 11 sensible brogues.

The only good tidings I can offer is that at last he seems to have found somewhere suited to his talents. Having renounced Christianity, Hinduism, Islam and Buddhism *et all*, he has been offered the post of Head of Religious Broadcasting for the BBC.

SOMETHING EXTRAORDINARY happened to me today which I must write down while it's fresh in my mind – although truth to tell, I don't think I'll ever forget the event if I live to be a hundred.

To begin at the beginning. I had been doing the rounds of my parish trying to drum up business, and had had quite a tiring day as can happen when most of them refuse even to open the door to you. Honestly, the times I've had to get down on my hunkers and shout through their letterboxes, 'You're all doomed. Would you rather live sin-filled lives that will lead you to damnation and everlasting torture in the flames of Hell than spend an hour or two with me?' And amazingly, they often shout back, 'Yes.' Actually, if I'm to be strictly accurate, they *always* shout back, 'Yes.' They seem to think that entering Heaven will be easy, but it's not. As the Bible says, 'It is easier for a camel to pass through the eye of a needle if it's dipped in a good quality oil first.' (I might have misquoted slightly there, I'll check up later on.)

Anyway, I was wondering whom to visit next when the rain started. It came down in buckets; I was soaked through in no time at all. That, coupled with the fact that the semi-permanent drip on my nose was no longer in evidence due to the wind being so strong and blowing against me it was pushing the offending liquid back up my nostrils and out through my tear ducts, made me feel that the day had been a complete waste of time.

Glancing at my watch, I noticed I had forgotten to put my watch on so I had no idea what the time was.

'Excuse me,' I said to a passer-by, 'I wonder if you could . . . ?'

He never even gave me the courtesy of looking my way. '*No,*' was all I got in reply.

As I stood there, thinking that my fellow human beings were maybe not worth my efforts to save them from themselves, a bus passed by and it seemed to me deliberately swerved so that

it would go right through an enormous black mass of rain
water, thus enveloping me in a wave of dirty, smelly, greasy,
petrol-stained puddle water. I think I heard the driver shout,
'Got him', and I *definitely* saw a small boy give me what I
can only describe as the sign of victory out of the back seat of
the bus.

I stood there, soaking wet, bereft of any sign that humanity
wanted to be saved, and bereft, it seemed to me, of any sign
that God wanted to save them. A down and out with a sandwich
board draped over a rain-sodden old herringbone coat
approached me. His body was bent over as he struggled to
make headway against the wind and driving rain. As he shuffled
his way towards me I could see that the text on the front of the
sandwich board said, in predictably large bold letters: THE
END IS NIGH. Despite my own feelings of misery and gloom
I was moved to lift this poor unfortunate's spirit and so I made
to offer him a cheery wave.

Something drew me to his eyes. They were barely visible, his
face being swathed in the folds of a thick brown scarf, but
nevertheless they fixed me with a stare that made the hairs on
the back of my neck rise.

He was mumbling to himself, his words struggling to
untangle themselves from the numerous folds of his scarf. As
he continued to stare, his left arm rose from his side and with
long expressive fingers he pointed straight at me. His voice
strangely high and shrill suddenly cut through the cold and
damp of the day, proclaiming 'For You The Dark Days are
Nearing!' Then it descended into a menace-laden whisper:
'Remember, Reverend. As You Sow, So Shall You Reap.
Remember. Remember.'

His voice tailed off as he left me staring at his back, the
memory of his eyes cold and cruel had swept my good
intentions aside and left me numbed and shocked. Why should
a complete stranger bear me such ill will? Why? Why? Why?

I could find no answer, so then and there I decided to call it a day, not only with my flock but also with my vocation. My very reason for living seemed to have been driven out of me.

In essence, I had for the first time ever lost not only my faith in mankind but also in my Creator. How could I continue to serve my ministry when it was patently obvious no one on Earth or in the Heavens gave a rat's bum. I truly felt an anguish that I did not think I was capable of. Indeed, I began to sob and cry, and as my tears flowed they mingled with the rain cascading down my cheeks and joined the drip from my nose (the wind had eased up a bit). With a heavy and leaden heart I trudged homewards, not knowing how I was going to break the terrible tidings to my dear wife; not knowing if she would understand, would offer sympathy with my plight, or indeed even want to continue to live with a man who now believed in . . . *nothing*.

Eventually the manse was in sight. Seeing the dull, grey, uninspiring box that we call home was for me always a moment that lifted my heart, but alas not this time. I started to pray that this blackness would be lifted from me, and then I remembered that I no longer believed in . . . Him.

On reaching the front door, I rang the doorbell and waited for it to chime out the old Salvation Army standard 'My Cup's Full and Running Over', which I'd had installed at no little expense. I was making a mental note to have it changed to 'The Party's Over' when I noticed that no sound came from the bell. Everything seemed to be conspiring to my *de profundis*. Drawing out the key from my water-filled pocket, I opened the door and entered the cold comfort of home.

I wanted to share my burden with Ephesia and called out her name.

'*Ephesia!*'

My desperate call rang through the air and cruelly came back to me unanswered.

'Oh God, where is she?' I asked myself. A sob escaped from

me. I realised once again that I was indeed asking myself . . . for I now knew there would be no response from You Know Who.

Along with the sobbing I started to shiver, which was not surprising considering I was soaked to the skin, so I determined to have a hot shower. At least that would be a respite from what had gone before. Shrugging off my wet things, I turned on the shower and waited for the hot water to come forth.

I began to hum for comfort to myself; it was the old hymn I'd first learned in the Lifeboys 'Will Your Anchor Hold in the Storms of Life?' Of course, I realised that I was reverting to some sort of religious poultice and was about to stop when I noticed something – something which was quite unbelievable, not to mention extremely frightening. *Someone else* was humming along with me.

I stopped humming and listened. Yes! There was without doubt another voice. But what was terrifying was, it was *not* *Ephesia's*. For a start it was in tune, and secondly it was masculine – although my dear wife has made the contralto part of the church choir her own (not a difficult task as she and I were the only ones in it). This voice had a deep resonance that discounted her from ownership.

My heart was racing as I tried to fathom out where it was coming from. I opened the bathroom door and listened in the hall; it was not coming from there. I now knew, beyond a shadow of a doubt, that the voice was definitely coming from the bathroom.

Opening the bathroom door I re-entered and was now out of my wits with fear. There was no one there but me . . . and the voice, which was now singing louder and also was no longer merely humming the tune but singing the words with a gusto that made my heart almost stop. This was undoubtedly some sort of sign for me in my hour of need and I had to find out who or, more frighteningly, what was the melodic messenger.

'Who's there?' I called and then, reverting to the years of

blind faith that I had always found a comfort in times of doubt, I cried out in hope, *'Is that you, my Saviour?'*

'Yes it is.' His voice seemed to fill the bathroom. I wanted to cry, 'Hallelujah!'

'Saviour, may I see you?'

'Afraid not,' was the answer, which was the one I expected anyway.

'Please do not stop singing, Saviour,' I pleaded.

'OK.' His wonderful voice once more filled the toilet and I almost danced with the joy of being there. All the worries of the day seemed to drop from me. At last I experienced true relief in the bathroom. Flushed with excitement, I luxuriated in harmonious happiness as his voice rang round, bouncing off the tiles and towels.

I began to wonder how I would cope with life if He left and the bathroom returned to the usage that it was designed for.

'Saviour?' I cried out.

'Yes.'

'Will you stay here forever?'

'No.'

'Will you be long?' (How many times had I said that before in connection with Ephesia's frequent bouts of constipation? Who knows, maybe this would be the miracle cure she'd been looking for?)

'Ten minutes.'

Panic rose in me. *'No! No! Don't leave me!'*

His voice was still singing, but it was no longer the Lifeboys' anchor song. He was now singing, 'Volare oh, oh . . . Cantare oh, oh, oh, oh'.

My head was spinning. *'Saviour, where are you? . . . Where are you, my Saviour?'*

'I'm down here.' His voice was like listening to birdsong as he continued singing, 'No wonder my happy heart sings, Your love has given me wings.'

I searched for the source that I might erect a shrine there when he left to go back to Heaven. Mercifully, it was not coming from the lavvy pan: *'Thanks for that, Saviour.'*

'Nae bother. La la la la la la la.'

I had to try to find him. To maybe gaze upon his radiance filled me with a joy that was unconstrained. I continued my search all round the floor: the washhand basin; the wee basket with all the soaps and shampoos that we'd brought back from hotels we'd stayed in; the shower cubicle. Then, as I approached the bath, my heart began to pound. The voice was definitely stronger in the *bath*. There was only one place it could be coming from.

'Saviour? Is that you down the plug hole?'

'Yes. I'll be another five minutes.'

At that moment, I heard the front door slam shut. I could tell from the particular squelching sound her wellies made that it was Ephesia.

'Ephesia! Come quick! I've found God.'

'Well, considering the fact that you are a minister, it's about time,' she responded.

'He's in here, in the bathroom,' I called out.

She arrived at the bathroom door, grabbed me by my nipples (I'd forgotten I had no clothes on) and said, 'How many dry sherries have you had?'

'No! No! Listen!' I implored. 'The Saviour is in here. He's down the plug hole. He was singing "Will Your Anchor Hold in the Storms of Life?", now he's changed it to "Volare". Listen.'

She gave me the most pitiful look and, with a scorn in her voice that seemed to come from somewhere deep within the darkest recesses of her being, she pronounced, 'That's not the Saviour singing. That's the plumber. He's down in the cellar clearing globules of your hair that are clogging up the drains. The water wouldn't drain away, I didn't know what to do, so I looked up a plumber in the *Yellow Pages*. He arrived about half an hour ago, said it was a block in the cellar drain and I left him to it while I went shopping.'

'But he answered to the name of "Saviour",' I exclaimed.

'He told me his mother and father are Spanish. His name's "Xavier", not "Saviour". *God*, what are you like? Cover yourself up before he comes up for payment.' Then, with a parting glare that made my manhood head for cover, she was off to the kitchen.

Despite Ephesia's scorn, I realised that something profound had just happened to me. There I was at the end of my tether; all love of life had left me, my faith gone, nothing left to live for. But I had been pulled back from the brink by a plumber; a common tradesman whose name was Spanish for 'saviour'. Was there not another tradesman, a carpenter, who had been sent by a father? Was not his name 'Saviour'? Did he not drive out the waste that had been clogging up the hearts of men? Coincidence? I think not.

MATTHEW 14, VERSE 43

Who hath ears to hear, let him hear.

On the other hand, I don't think Jesus ever sang 'Volare'.

TOMORROW IS VALENTINE'S DAY and I can't decide what to get Ephesia. Last year was an unmitigated disaster. I passed a florist which advised 'Say It with Flowers', so that's what I did. When they arrived, she flew into a rage. Unfortunately, I had unwittingly sent her a bouquet of pee the beds. I never knew why they were called that until I smelled the bouquet coming from the bouquet. I think they should rename them 'cat's piss'. I offered to swap them for toilet water; that just made it worse.

'Have you got a bladder fixation?' she was screaming at me.

She was still a wee bit upset and offering me a 'square go' when I got a phone call from a colleague – I would have said 'friend', except he's the minister who married us. There was a bit of a panic on the wedding day because he was over an hour late. However, eventually the deed was done.

'Do you remember when I gave you that awful fright?' he said on the phone.

'Yes,' I replied, 'I'm still married to her.'

I decided to take her out for a meal to see if that would ease the tension caused by the flower debacle. So I asked, 'Would you like to eat, my sweetheart?'

'Why would I want to eat your sweetheart?' She was obviously in the mood for an argument.

'I meant, would you like to go out to a restaurant?'

'Oh! I see. My cooking is no longer good enough! Between my dreadful cooking and my incessant bed-wetting, it's a wonder that you put up with me at all.'

I could sense she was about to drone on forever. Trying to halt the Harpy when she has the high moral ground is never an easy task. Wheedling is always an option I grasp with both hands on these occasions.

'My God! You look ravishing when you're angry. Your eyes sparkle! Your skin glows! And your lips are moist.' Actually, her eyes were watering, her face was sweaty and her mouth was salivating, but better a white lie than a black eye, as they say.

We went to an enchanting restaurant that I always use. The food's terrible, the service is worse, and the kitchen looks like a scene from *The Killing Fields*, but it suits me because it's cheap.

The waiters finally gave up arguing over who would serve us and one of them approached our table. I was not enamoured with him because the last time we were in there we actually had to make the old joke complaint that there was a dead fly in my soup.

He said, 'I know. I think it's the hot water that kills them. D'you want me to swap it for a live one? Be a bit fresher anyway. It's manky as well. I'll get you a clean one.'

This time I decided to steal a march on him. As he approached I said, 'Are your flies clean?'

'They are noo,' he countered, wiping the front of his trousers with a serviette. 'What brings you in the night?'

'I'm in because of an unfortunate choice of flora,' I explained.

'You didnae do too well wi' Ephesia either, did you?' he scoffed. Ignoring him, I said grace:

Oh Lord, we thank you for the meal to come,

Your bounty's truly universal.

We know, dear Lord, it's not your fault

It's being delivered by this aircehole!

Beneath the table I felt Ephesia squeeze my knee. I think she quite likes it when I use the vernacular. Maybe I'll get her some perfume this year. I know she likes that Odey Colone, or is it Boady Colone? Or is it Soady Scone Colone? Or maybe it's Lily of the Marlene?

MY BROTHER RANALD contacted me this morning. I'll rephrase that. He didn't so much contact me as lie in wait for me.

To try and stop the constant nagging by my conscience that I was being indolent and not applying myself to solving the Synod's ultimatum, I'd been visiting my parents, now in their late eighties, still proud and self-reliant, refusing to be dependent on anyone – even me, their first begotten. They call me their ill-begotten, but I know they're only saying that because they're ancient, decrepit and wandering a bit. I adore them both.

Mere words can never describe the way I feel about my father. When I was just a wee tot my mother would tuck me up with a bedtime story, then kiss me goodnight leaving a lit candle so I would not be frightened, because like most kiddies I was afraid of the dark. I used to keep my eye fixed on that candle and feel comforted by its friendly glow, guttering gently and casting shadows all round the bedroom.

But there was one night that stands out, and to this day I can still wake up screaming in terror at the memory. Mummy had kissed me goodnight and, as I lay watching my friendly candle casting shadows on the wall, I became transfixed. My gaze was focusing on one particular shadow that was metamorphosing even as I stared. It seemed to move independently of the other shadows, as if obeying its own laws of physics and not the natural laws of this Earth.

Slowly it began to take on a shape that even to my tender years was frighteningly familiar. Fear rose up and filled my throat so that, desperate as I was and longing to shout for help, no real sound escaped, only a gasp of horror. What I could see on the wall was undoubtedly a *head*, affixed with what I knew to be the horns of *Lucifer himself*.

My wee body stiffened and became rigid as I watched two hands slowly take shape from what had been a black shapeless mass. They grew bigger as they seemed to stretch out of the wall towards me, and as if from the bowels of Hell itself I heard an unearthly chuckle which gurgled and hissed and finally crackled into a demonic frenzy of laughter.

I was about to pass out with fear when the light snapped on and my father filled the room, driving all the demons away. I can still hear his big masculine voice say to me, 'Got you that time, you wee bugger,' as he stood there with a Viking's helmet on and both hands encased in those tools for picking up leaves in the garden.

What a sense of humour he had. Even Ranald did not escape Daddy's devastating wit. There was the time Ranald was caught with some pals having a fly wee puff at a cigarette in the garden shed. Daddy accidentally walked in and discovered them passing this one cigarette around. Of course, they all panicked and were fulsome – maybe even grovelling – in their haste to apologise.

'Listen,' said father, with a mischievous glint in his eye. 'If you want to smoke, well that's alright, but do it in front of me, Ranald, not behind my back. OK?'

Ranald acquiesced with a sheepish nod of his head, his pals following suit.

'Right,' said my father. 'It's ridiculous that you're all sharing that one wee cigarette.' At that, he drew out his pipe, his thick black tobacco and his box of Swan Vestas matches. 'Do you fancy really smoking?'

'Aye, Mr Jolly,' they chorused, their faces lighting up with the anticipation of the pipe lighting up too.

'Righty ho!' said my father, putting the pipe to his mouth.

Licking his lips then letting them snap apart with a *smack* of sheer enjoyment, he lit a match, drew luxuriously on his pipe and threw the lit match on to a pile of oily rags – which immediately burst into flame and started the straw that the boys had been lying on to smoulder and catch fire also. And as the flames licked up the walls of the wooden shed, father

skipped outside and, roaring with laughter as he locked the
door, shouted out, '*Smoke away . . . Smoke away!*' He was still
chortling merrily to the sound of screaming and broken glass as
the boys threw themselves through the shed window. Aye,
when father was born they threw the mould away. However,
I digress.

As I was saying, Ranald contacted me as I was leaving Mum
and Dad's place. Just as I got to their front gate, he popped out
from behind a rhododendron bush, mugged me, stole all my
money and left me for dead. But typical Ranald. As I lay there
in a heap on the ground, he ruffled my hair, wiped my blood
off his hands on the rhododendron bush and, with a cheery
grin, said, 'Love to Ephesia', then off he went, with not a care
in the world, singing, 'When Somebody Loves You, It's No
Good Unless They Love You All the Way'.

People say Ranald takes after Daddy. I don't see it myself.

D EUTERONOMY 3, VERSE 1
*Then we turned and went up the way to Bashan: and Og
the king of Bashan came out against us, he and all his
people, to battle at Edrie.*

What do these words mean to us today? Well, I haven't a
clue. When I first heard the passage I thought that somebody
had went up a hill and a woman called Ann was getting bashed
by the people of Airdrie. However, these words came to
mind when I was re-reading a college report I'd got while I
was studying for the ministry from my old theology master,
Deuteronomy MacBride (or Ronnie, as we used to call him,
thereby waggishly shortening his first name). I postulated
this explanation to Ronnie and his reply made me pause for
reflection. He studied me for what seemed like an age, but was
probably only quite a long time, then smiling indulgently he
suggested to me I was like a partly empty vessel waiting to be
filled with the heady brew of knowledge – or, as he put it,
'You're no' the full cup of tea, are you?'

Deuteronomy MacBride was an unusual theology master.
His approach to the subject was different from all the other
tutors.

'Tell me, Jolly, what would be your answer if I told you that
I didn't believe in God *per se*?'

'My name's not Percy,' I ventured.

Deuteronomy's eyes looked up at the sky, and shaking his
head he expostulated, 'God, you're stupid.'

'You shouldn't talk to God like that,' I told him. 'He can't be
that stupid if he built the world in only six days. I once had to
build a set of drawers from B&Q and it was so hard I gave up
after a fortnight. So God can't be stupid to have built what he
did, *and* he didn't even have an instruction manual to look at.'

'Well, he can't be that bright if he made you,' said Ronnie
with what sounded like a rising tone of ire in his voice. 'In fact,'
he continued, 'listening to you, it's possible that single-handedly

you could convert the entire world . . . to atheism.'

I wasn't quite sure what an 'athe' was, so I said defensively, 'Aye, well, if it's His wish that we become atheisms, so be it.'

Deuteronomy seemed to be caught out by my logic, because losing all control he grabbed me by the throat and growled, 'Are you taking the piss?' I could tell by the way his face was reddening and the veins were starting to bulge from his neck in a most unusual shade of blue that this was not a rhetorical question. 'Because if you are, I'm warning you, I'm liable to do something you'll regret a lot more than I will.'

At that moment the door of his study opened and our principal the Very Reverend Obediah Lick popped his head round the door.

'Sorry to interrupt you while you're strangling Jolly, but I wondered if you could give me a lift into town? Cathy needs picked up from the station and my car's out of action.' Cathy was the principal's wife and indeed I always thought it a bit strange that the Very Reverend Lick should have a wife named Cathy. 'Do you want a hand to batter some sense into him?' the Very Reverend Lick offered, taking off his coat and rolling up his sleeves.

'Yes, thanks Obediah,' said Deuteronomy, 'and as soon as we're finished I'll run you into town.'

'Right then, let's get to it,' said the Very Reverend Lick, pummelling me with left and right jabs to the body. He started to laugh, 'I suppose this is me Licking him into shape.'

'Oh! Nice one, Obediah,' chortled Deuteronomy, sticking his boot up my sit-upon. 'Watch you don't hurt yourself punching him with no proper gloves on, Obediah!' he puffed, straining himself in his efforts to rearrange my rectum.

I'm sorry to say I passed out before the lesson ended, but I know that my two old tutors made the effort to set me on the right path, no matter how much they suffered physically while they were pounding the word of the Almighty into my own pain-wracked body.

They were admittedly hard at the time, but the grounding in solid theology I received has stayed with me to this day, as have the bruises. Indeed, in times of self-doubt I often remember the words: 'And the apostle John said unto Simon called Peter, "What is your name anyway?"'

If further proof be needed of the wisdom imparted to me by those two wonderful men then I offer my experience of just last week when a non-believer asked me how I could say for certain there was a God. I replied, 'Because I've read His book.'

I could have added, 'And someday I hope He'll autograph it for me.'

S OMETIMES I FIND that I have given so much time to my flock that I forget how much my own family misses me. So I phoned my mother and father to tell them that, for a wee treat, I was coming over to cheer them up. Of course, they both know how busy I can get and are always selflessly saying that they are doing very well without me coming over and spoiling their day, but they have the same off-the-wall sense of fun as me, so I take no notice.

Both the parents are getting on a bit now, but that hasn't curtailed their activities and, despite the fact that they are in their late eighties, they still keep up their hobbies. Mother's is making cups of tea, falling asleep in her chair (or, indeed, anywhere that will support her weight) and talking to my father even although he never listens to her. Father has always been keen on annoying people and is very good, not to say excellent at it. He should be, of course, because he annoyed mother day and night until he got so good at it she used to say he annoyed her just by being there.

Father always said, 'If you're going to do something, make sure you do it properly.' He used to practice annoyance techniques on Ranald and I when we were young, with exercises such as tying the hairs on our heads together with waxed string so that we had to walk down the road to school with our heads stuck to each other. Twice we were kidnapped by travelling freak shows and offered lucrative contracts to join on a full-time basis. We always declined, but father used to say it was always an avenue that was open to us if we found ourselves unemployable. As he frequently did.

I always looked forward to my impromptu visits. I say 'impromptu' because I noticed that if I gave them more than a day's notice, they always pretended they had moved house. Such was their sense of fun, they once hired two bouncers to move me off the premises. Heady stuff indeed.

Opening the front gate I looked around for the inherent

booby-traps father invariably set for me. Just in time I noticed the trip-wire that was concealed in the undergrowth that passed for a pathway. With a wry grin I spied some leaves heaped up just beyond the trip-wire. They were there so that when you stepped over the trip-wire thinking you were safe, *bang*, you were caught in the mantrap hidden amongst the innocent-looking pile of leaves. As I stepped around the leaves I shook my head; he was sadly beginning to lose some of his former sharpness. A year ago he would have been subtler. More, what was the word? More . . . That was when I fell down the eight-foot hole he had dug.

'Got you, you pile of dogs' doings!' he guffawed from behind the World War Two Bofors gun he had camouflaged as a pergola. You can't imagine the feeling of pride that was welling up inside me as I lay there nursing what I suspected might have been a broken ankle.

An hour later, as I sat with my ankle wrapped in a packet of frozen peas to reduce the swelling, mother gave me my fourth cup of tea and asked me for the fourth time, 'How many sugars do you take in your tea?'

I told her again, for the fourth time, 'I don't take sugar.'

'That's right. Neither you do,' she nodded, putting a box of matches into an empty tea cup and stirring them with a boiled egg. 'How does that taste?'

'Well,' I said, 'although I don't take sugar, I do take boiling water and tea.'

'Instead of sugar?' she asked incredulously. 'You were never brought up to do that in this house. That'll be Euphonia and her Fancy Dan ways that's got you into that habit. Did I ask you if you wanted a cup o' tea?'

My father was now about to light up his pipe. As one of his annoying habits, this was up there with the best because the thick, acrid smoke that belched forth was guaranteed to send everyone into a fit of near uncontrollable coughing, not to mention a stinging in your eyes that could take a week to clear up. He used to call it *'the clincher'*.

'Where are the matches?' he enquired with the hint of battle in his eyes.

'I don't know,' said mother tetchily.

'They're here in my tea cup, under the boiled egg,' I interjected with some trepidation.

'You're losing the plot,' said my father, shaking his head and giving me a glance of barely disguised contempt.

'You leave him alone, you,' said my mother. 'Do you want a cup o' tea, son? It'll help you wash down that boiled egg.'

'No thanks, mother,' I replied. 'Can I get you one?' She didn't reply because she was asleep.

'She's no' sleeping. She's just pretending to sleep so I'll think I'm no' annoying her when I light up my pipe, thereby annoying me,' my father informed me smugly. 'But I know her tricks, she cannae beat The Master.'

Fixing his gaze on her, he lit up his pipe. Drawing in air with a gurgling, wet, swooshing sound, he started to discharge plumes of dark, evil-smelling, foul, rancid smoke that seemed to seek you out and attack you like an Exocet missile. In no time I was engulfed and retching. However, I was not the game my father was after. Mother was still out to the world, her jaw slack and relaxed, and a tell-tale dribble of wet at the corners of her mouth confirmed that her snores were genuine. As I was heading for the safe haven of the garden I could hear my father shouting as he stood over her inert, somnambulant figure, blowing clouds of smoke directly up her nose and into her face, 'You're just doing it to annoy me. Well, I'm no' annoyed at all. I'm perfectly calm . . . *Cough, damn you . . . cough.*'

I decided to call it a day and leave the two lovebirds. Quietly drawing the door closed I hobbled down the stairs, musing on the certain fact that it was their parental guidance that had formed me into what I had become today. Or, as someone once said, 'If you want a place in the sun, you've got to put up with a few blisters.'

Fortified with the momentum of my visit, I determined to renew my efforts to swell my little flock and so make father and mother as proud of me as I was of them. I was so determined that I decided to put it off till tomorrow so I could give it all my attention.

Monday, 10.00 a.m.

I know that building up my 'fan base' – as the business whizz-kids would say – is going to be a little bit difficult. Still, I've never in my life been a quitter and I don't intend to start now. So let's get down to it, Jolly, just how are we going to solve this problem?

Monday, 2.30 p.m.

Isn't it amazing how long you can sit without a single idea entering your head. Wait a minute, I know what I'll do . . . I'll go and put the kettle on. Maybe that will lead to inspiration.

Monday, 4 p.m.

I'll put the kettle on again, see if it'll work this time.

Tuesday, 6.45 a.m.

Still nothing.

Tuesday, 10.00 p.m.

Right, I've given it my best shot. I'm packing it in.

Wednesday, 10.00 a.m.

I awoke about seven-ish and lay awake hoping to give birth to some kind of bright idea from my barren brain. Then, as if by Immaculate Conception, I had a flash of inspiration. And considering who my boss is, why not?

I'd turned on the television and after about five minutes had turned it off again, having had enough of the smug, sofa-bound presenters of what is now called 'news' shuffling about and trying to convince you that what they're saying actually matters a jot. And trying to inveigle you into their sordid world by exhorting you to *phone* us, or *text* us or *e-mail* us or, if you're totally doo-lally, *write* to us, but whatever you do please don't *ignore us!* Then, having promoted this idea for the entire running-time of the programme, they end by apologising for not reading any of it out because they've run out of time.

In desperation I switched on the wireless, which is equally annoying but at least you don't have to look at them. Newspapers I find are the best because you don't have to look at them or listen to them, and their opinions can be relegated to the side of the toilet pan so long as you're not expecting visitors. I was just about to switch the radio off as well when the announcer announced the morning programme's 'Thought for Today'. Now, it used to be a member of the clergy who gave their thoughts out to the masses, but these days anybody who has a thought of any kind can air their opinions on the . . . eh? Air. This morning it was a musician from The American Church of People Who Like to Hum Hymns. She said – with the monotone that seems to be mandatory to some Americans – that the membership was growing every day because although people liked the tunes, they couldn't be bothered to learn the words. Consequently, her church was experiencing phenomenal growth and you could easily tell one of their congregation as they were usually humming.

It goes without saying that I found this idea entirely pertinent to my own parish due to the fact that most of them had been humming for years. There and then I decided to adopt this idea and audition for hummers to perform in the church choir.

How to advertise the auditions was my next concern. I had long ago given up the parish magazine as it was becoming commercially non-viable due to the fact that the cheapest print run was 20,000 and we were only managing to shift four copies. Two of those were to Ephesia and I, and the other two were freebies. On top of that, we had to pay the city cleansing department twenty quid to come and take the remaining 19,996 copies away, so that is definitely out.

I've decided to place a card in the window of the local newsagent and find out what the response is. I believe the phrase is 'testing the market'. In this case it could be more like 'hunting the hummers'.

The next task is going to be what to say and how to say it. Hmm.

After only two days I've composed the document.

POP IDOLS AUDITIONS

Think you have the voice to make it big in the music business? Then come to the Church Hall on Wednesday the 18th at 8 p.m. Ability to read music not necessary.

(In fact, considering they were just going to hum, the ability to read words was not necessary either.) This was giving a week's notice, which should be sufficient.

The newsagent proprietor, Mr Majid (pronounced 'Maheed'), was very amenable and in fact insisted there would be no charge.

'Thanks very much, Mr Majid,' I replied. 'Please feel free to join us any time at services.' He is a lovely man and insisted I call him by his first name, Hamaffa.

I have prevailed upon Ephesia to help me judge the event, and of course she has been wonderfully supportive – her only condition being that the contralto spot was hers. She will also naturally gravitate towards the prima donna position so in essence, that will be two birds for the price of one. And as the old saying goes, 'A bird in the hand can give you a trill'. This is especially apt with Ephesia as she has a vibrato that could switch an egg.

I'm beginning to revel in my role of empressario and really think I can be the new Pete Waterboy – but in a closer-to-God kind of way. Roll on the 18th.

The 18th, 11 p.m.

The auditions were not what I would call a total failure in so far as there was a wonderful response to my notice in Mr Majid's. Indeed, there were queues of auditionees right round the corner. Where it all fell apart was when the first songster rendered the first song. He was maybe about twelve – or it could have been thirty, it was hard to tell as his face was hidden beneath what looked like a cleaning woman's mop under a tea cosy. His face was mostly covered in what I took to be silver curtain rings, and the bit of his face that was visible suggested that his skin was riveted on with plukes. He said he was very influenced by Bob Marley. I really couldn't see that what kind of pills he was feeding his dog on was of relevance to the auditions and told him so. He gave me this strange look and then asked me if I had something against Rasta. I assured him I'd never even met the man, never mind had a grudge against him. Then he asked me what kind of music I was into. I said I liked hymns.

'Who?' he asked.

'What?' I asked, puzzled.

'Who's he?' he asked.

'Who's who?' I asked back.

'Him?' he said.

'Who?' I said.

'Him?' he said again.

'Him who?'

'Him that you said you liked?' he shouted.

'I didn't say I liked him,' I said. 'I said I liked *hymns,*' I shouted back.

'Oh! Is there two o' them?' he said.

'*Look, I like hymns. Is that so hard to understand?*' I was starting to lose it slightly.

'No,' he nodded. 'I prefer women myself, but if you're into group sex wi' men, cool, man, that's up to you. All's I want to know is what kind of song yez would like me to sing?'

I decided to stop trying to have anything resembling a sensible conversation with him and told him I would like him to hum a hymn.

'You've lost me completely, pal,' he said, shaking his head and looking at me as if I was not of this Earth.

'Dear God, help me.' I was now quite close to sobbing with frustration. '*Look*. I just want to hear you hum 'O Come All Ye Faithful'. Alright? *That's* all I want you to do. OK? Think you can do that simple task?'

He looked perplexed. 'Eh! – is that no' a hymn? Are you expectin' me to hum a hymn?'

'*Yes! Yes! At last the penny has dropped. Thank you, God. Thank you,*' I howled on bended knees.

'Eh! Haud on a minute, you advertised for pop idols. Pop doesnae mean hymns. I'm going to sue you under the Trade's Description Act. Just what do you think "pop" means?' he snapped, thrusting his face into mine with a jangling sound as his curtain rings clanged off of each other.

I was definitely cornered and I knew it. Then it came to me – divine inspiration saved me again – this time from a possible lawsuit.

'"Pop" means,' I said, with a smugness I found hard to hide, '"Performances of Psalms".'

There was quite a substantial pause before he addressed himself to me. Finally he nodded.

'Respect, man. You're totally weird, but respect to you – and your boyfriends.'

Of course, once he had passed the word down the line that I was a gay vicar who was looking for group sex whilst humming 'O Come All Ye Faithful', I was sunk without a trace. Every one of the potential psalmists disappeared. Except for one, who turned up late thereby missing the slur on my sexuality. His name is Darius and he seems quite keen.

Thursday 20th
9.00 a.m.

Someone phoned. The line was very bad, but I think they said 'I'm going to get you.' Obviously a wrong number. Apart from that, not a lot happened today.

Thursday 20th
11.15 p.m.

IT NEVER CEASES TO AMAZE ME how the lay person assumes that we members of the clergy are pigeon-holed into modes of behaviour that seem to fit the stereotypical behaviour that we are fitted into when we are pigeon-holed into this behavioural way of behaving. If you see what I mean.

Take, for example, my good friend the Roaming Catholic priest Father John Knox. This Catholic pastor does not fit into the public expectations of how a priest should behave. He doesn't gamble, drink to excess, or threaten his parishioners with the Bad Fire if they happen to eat a Lorne sausage on a Friday. He's not Irish, and he doesn't support the Glasgow Celtic Football Club. His parish is almost as weakly attended as my own. In fact, when he visits his flock he is as welcome as a burnt iron-mark on the back of your underpants.

He seems to revel in this off-the-wall way of conducting his ministry. About the only thing that identifies him with his priesthood is the black suit, black trilby hat and wrap-around white collar that he takes great pride in wearing. The other thing that marks him out as an oddity is that he supports Partick Thistle Football Club. So you can see that Father Knox certainly proves my point about stereotypes.

He tells the story of setting out to go and support Partick Thistle one Saturday.

He was standing at the bus stop in his usual garb of black suit, collar and trilby when a taxi pulled up and the door opened. Inside were three football fans who he could see by the scarves and rosettes were obviously supporters of Glasgow Celtic.

'Jump in, Father,' they shouted, holding the door of the taxi open. 'We're going up to Parkhead to see the Celtic.'

This was like a red rag to a bull to Father Knox. 'I don't like Celtic. And I'm not going to Parkhead. In fact, I wouldn't be seen dead in the place. I'm going to Firhill to see the Thistle,' he said proudly.

'Oh, sorry!' was the reply. 'We thought you were a priest.' At that the taxi door was slammed shut and it sped off. Would you credit it?

Another good friend I have in the ecclesiastic side of life is Rabbi Arrafat. I have been to three karaoke nights for the Friends of World Fatwahs and not once have I heard him sing 'My Yiddisha Mamma' or 'Hava Nagila'. In fact, I don't think he would even know what a Nagila was, and he's certainly never offered me one. And what about my other friend who is a member of the Hindu faith. He is a right holy fakir, but when he goes upstairs to his bedroom he doesn't climb up a rope, he uses the stairs like you and I would. And you can also lie on his bed without a years' supply of Elastoplast to stop the flow of blood from the nails.

It really is quite ridiculous the impression that the laity have of us. We were all at our monthly night out – which this year was held by the Hare Krishna Hair Restoration Salon and Heavy Metal Music Appreciation Society – and the conversation turned to this very subject. Everyone was giving instances of how the stereotypes were way off the mark, and I was also saying how unfair it all was.

'Scottish ministers are always being portrayed as dour, dreich, out-of-touch and humourless, long lumps of misery. I've even been accused of that myself,' I smirked. 'Could you believe it?'

I think there must have been something wrong with the dinner because to a man all of them started choking on their food.

I DECIDED TO GO TO THE BARBER'S TODAY as I was starting to look quite unkempt. Ephesia always lets me know when it's time to get my hair cut. After I've washed my hair, she gathers up the floating follicles which have clogged round the plug hole and throws them at me. It just goes to illustrate how, when you've shared your life with someone for as long as we have, often you don't need words to communicate, you can sense what the other is thinking.

Over the years I have to say that her aim has improved beyond all expectations. When she first took to throwing my hair at me I became aware that she tended to throw it with a bias which made it veer to the right. She did not allow for the fact that I always ducked to the left, thereby causing her to miss. This became a bit of a game, which I have to admit I enjoyed more than Ephesia. It also had the added bonus of giving our wallpaper that hessian look that was so popular at the time. Ephesia, however, got very angry when a parishioner remarked that it was the first time she had seen hessian wallpaper suffering from alopecia. She instinctively knew that something was amiss with her throwing technique, so she cleverly corrected this by throwing it with a bias that made it veer to the left. I, of course, counteracted by simply swaying to the right, thereby causing the remains of the recently washed and now bedraggled barnet to miss its mark again.

I always remember, it was a Tuesday I got my comeuppance. I had complemented her on her birds' nest soup that evening during dinner. 'What *is* that subtle flavouring?' I enquired.

'Essence of Brylcream mixed with eau de Vosene,' she cackled.

After that I stopped ducking and gave in to the fact that I should get my hair cut when it hit me.

As I was strolling down to the barbers once again I tried to think how I could boost the congregation and appease my masters. Always on the lookout for lapsed members, I was passing by old Mr Crabbit's house and saw he was out tending to his garden. This was his pride and joy and he spent countless hours in it, searching for a weed that would be foolish enough to try and elude him. When he did find one, he used to tar and feather it and then nail it to a tree 'as a warning', he said.

Thoughts that I might inveigle him back to the Church made the evangelist in me tingle with the possibility of conversion. I noticed he was on his hands and knees and his hands were slowly exploring the lawn. His face was just above the sward and the study of rapt concentration as he scanned his kingdom of grass was so tangible that you could feel it. Figuring that a wee bit of flattery can get you anywhere, I approached him with a wave of the hand and a disarming smile.

'It's so nice to see you, Mr Crabbit. Is this you looking for weeds, then?' I beamed.

'Bugger,' he blasphemed. 'You've made me lose count. I'll need to start all over counting this grass again. God but you're an annoying swine of a man.'

By the tone of his language it was obvious that he was in need of spiritual guidance as soon as possible. Not only his language, but the fact he was actually counting the blades of grass on his lawn suggested that he might not just be spiritually bereft, it could be that the elevator was not going up to the top floor as well. I judged it was better to keep on the flattery tack.

'You know,' I said. 'Looking at this wonderful garden, with its gently rolling and verdant banks of beautifully tended lawn; the cornucopia of flowers; those big yellow ones, and the red ones . . .' (I'm not very good with the names of flowers) '. . . that are just behind the kind of purpley bluey ones. Not to mention the variety of trees that you have. I can only marvel at God's great plan.'

'Really,' he said. 'Well, you want to have seen the mess it was in when He had it a' tae Hisself.'

I decided to laugh off this piece of blasphemy and carry on with my attempted conversion.

79

'Ha, ha!' I laughed. 'And tell me, what are those crimson, white and orange ones over there?'

'That's the wife's knickers. You're looking at the washing line,' he barked, 'and I'm no' comin' back to your church, so you can forget it.'

'If you think I came over here just to try to get you to come to my church, you're sadly mistaken,' I lied.

'You're a liar,' he said.

'I am not,' I lied again.

'You've just lied again,' he said.

'I certainly have not,' I lied for the third time. A cock crowed in the distance, which was a miracle because there were no farms within a fifty-mile radius. I thought, maybe God's telling me I'm pushing the boat out here, change the subject. 'If I gave you money, would you come back to the church?' I said, but not in a wheedling, I've-lost-all-control-of-myself sort of way (oh no, I'm lying again).

The look in his eyes was one of scorn. 'You should be ashamed of yourself. You, a man of the cloth, offering people money to come to your church. You make me sick. How much will you give me, then?'

'A quid,' I said.

'Five.'

'Two quid.'

'Four, then.'

'Settle on three?'

'Done.' He held his hand out. I shook it. 'When do I get the three quid?' he enquired.

'After church on Sunday.'

'You're no' lying again, are you?'

'Of course not,' I lied again, but this time it didn't count because unknown to him I'd crossed my fingers behind my back, thus nullifying all that I had said. I was not about to dismiss the hint that I'd got from God. But he was looking at me as if trying to see whether my intentions were as truthful as I had made out. I was starting to colour up, which Ephesia has told me is always a sign that I'm in white untruth mode.

'Oh, is that a weed?' I cried out in horror, pointing to the far side of the garden.

Before I could blink he was off, his trowel springing into his hand like a gunslinger from the old Wild West looking to shoot the bad guy. Which might not be too far off the mark when he doesn't get his three quid after church on Sunday. I determined to make my sermon such a clarion call for compassion that he would forget his anger and be filled with the spirit of Christianity and charity and that love for his fellow beings would permeate and bring him to the joy of true fulfilment. However, maybe I'd better bring the three quid along as well.

My instinct told me that now was the time to slip away, while old Crabbit was otherwise occupied. I could hear him challenging the imaginary weed to, 'Show yourself like a man. Come on, I'll give you a square go, just you and me, a fair fight till one of us is dead.' Yes, it was definitely a good time to exit.

However, as I turned away I could not help but notice two small boys crouching behind the wall that separated the Crabbit garden from the street. They were, in fact, only about ten feet from him but hidden from his view by the wall.

He had just finished his tirade and had turned his back to have another go at me, when one of the boys shouted out in a high squeaky voice, 'Away, ya mug.'

Spinning round on his heels, he screamed at the non-existent weed, 'Who're you calling a mug?'

Sensing that this might be a lengthy argument between him and the apprentice ventriloquists, I started off to the barbers. Passing Mr Majid's newsagents, I was about to enter and buy a newspaper when I remembered that the barber always had papers lying around so his customers would not be tempted to leave should they have to wait. I was immediately cheered up by the thought that I had just saved at least forty pence. Also, I could catch up on what the ordinary man in the street thought about life, politics and current events. Indeed, the whole rich tapestry that was the modern way of living was mine to explore simply by having a read at *The Sun*. Also, by studying the paper, I might just be able to tap into a way to swell the congregation, which was my main concern. Of course, that would mean I would be exposed to the inevitable display of some young, succulent and nubile female bodies shamelessly displaying their firm breasts and flawless flesh, but I would just have to grit my teeth and see that through.

I now had a spare forty pence burning a hole in my pocket which I was about to squander. Ephesia says she hates this reckless side of my personality, but I have a sneaking suspicion that she can get a wee bit excited by the odd display of wantonness that I am prone to.

Mr Majid's shop is a typical family newsagents. A Lotto machine lurks alluringly in the far corner next to the exotic magazine section. From here the eye is led over to the video section where there is a wide variety of videos to choose from, such as *Driller Killers, I was a Teenage Vampire Drug Addict* (the director's cut), *A Beginner's Guide to Group Sadism, Bob The Builder* and a whole host of others that seem to cater for practically every member of the family. From there you can then wander lazily to the greetings card section, where you can buy a card for all occasions, providing it's for a birthday. As you progress past the grocery stands with their tins of, well, anything that could be crammed into a tin, I suppose, you can then test your reflexes by the physically challenging experience of trying to skip your way over and round about the marvellous assortment of empty cardboard boxes that had once proudly contained exotic flavoured crisps or, indeed, any kind of food you craved, providing it's wrapped up in some kind of plastic. Then, on to where Mr Majid is invariably going through his till, separating the various monetary denominations and waiting with his lovely smile that makes you feel you are always welcome. There is an iron grill separating him from any physical contact with his customers, which is a wise precaution on Mr Majid's part.

'I gave you something for the church roof fund last week,' he joked, slamming the till shut and sliding down the little wire door on his protective grill where he accepted your money. 'And I've told you that I can't join your congregation due to the fact that I don't want to be bored out of my skull.'

We always had this banter between us so I countered with the witty retort of, 'Oh?'

I had obviously triumphed in this battle of ripostes because he just shook his head and went back to his currency-counting.

'Eh! What could I get for that?' I said, plonking down the forty pence.

He regarded the cash thoughtfully. 'Well, for another ten pence I could let you have a half-share in a Lotto ticket, but I don't suppose you approve of gambling?' It wasn't so much gambling I disapproved of, it was losing I was dead against, so I was not about to blow the lot on a game of chance.

'Eh! No. That's right enough,' I hedged, trying to avoid looking him in the eye.

'How about a bar of chocolate, a packet of crisps, chewing gum? Any of those tempt you?'

My head shook as I shrugged my shoulders in a dismissive manner. 'Not really.'

'A newspaper?'

Once again my head answered for me.

'Well, apart from a single Brillo Pad, that's about it.'

My ears pricked up at this and a shiver ran up my spine. I knew that I had just had one of those life-changing moments that confirmed my chosen calling. Here I was, caught in the clutches of Mammon, wanting to lavish this money that had unexpectedly been granted to me – on myself. Mr Majid had shown me that there was another way open. Why not spend the money on a gift for Ephesia?

Sliding the money beneath the grill I said, 'I'll take the Brillo Pad.'

I watched him as he slid off the stool he was perched on and went in search of Ephesia's gift. I knew that he had probably no idea of the momentous occurrence that had just happened in his very shop. To him it was not of great import. But to me, I could see a greater hand at work than the one which was currently handing me a Brillo Pad wrapped in a poke.

I shook his hand and, staring through the rather thick lenses on his spectacles into his eyes – and, I suspect, his very soul – I smiled and whispered, 'Out of the mouths of babes and innocents, eh? My wife and I both thank you.'

As I left the shop I could hear him say under his breath what sounded like, 'atoe taluney'. I don't speak Asian but I suspect it's some sort of blessing.

With a smile now playing around the corners of my mouth, I headed for the barbers with the thought that Ephesia would be doubly pleased. Not only would she not have to hit me with the hair from the plug hole but she had a present to open up as well. How many husbands *say it with Brillo Pads*? As my favourite magician would say, 'Not a lot.'

The bell trilled out behind the door of the owner, old Robert Sinparsley. 'Scissors R Us' was the name above the door and underneath in gold lettering was 'Proprietor R. Sinparsley'. He was not a tremendously busy barber due to the fact that he was looked upon as being a bit old-fashioned, but at fifty pence for a haircut he could always rely on my custom. I usually gave him a fiver to himself as a tip (that's pence, of course) – I'm afraid if you want good service you have to stump up these days. I hoped my face did not register the disappointment that I felt when I saw there was no one else waiting, thus depriving me of a free read at his newspapers.

'Right, minister. Sit yourself down on the box,' he said, pointing to the newly painted, upturned orange box that he used instead of a barber's chair. 'I've been on a course that's brought me up to scratch with the new-fangled haircuts that are on the go just now,' he explained, poking at the inside of his ear with the leg of his spectacles. 'I thought it was about time for a wee refresher course,' he intoned, dislodging some offending wax and wiping it off the leg of his specs on to his barber's coat. 'Aye! If you don't move wi' the times, you're dead meat in this game.' He nodded sagely while wrapping an old tablecloth round my neck. 'So what would you like? A number one or a number two?'

'I've already been to the bathroom,' I explained.

'That's just as well seeing as how we don't have a cludgie on the premises. However, I think the confusion here arises from the fact that you are not aware that a number one and number two alludses to the type of baldy that is in style. Number one'll leave you wi' a head like a ball-bearing, whereas your number two will leave you wi' a head like a ball-bearing that's ran over the top o' some iron filings. Number three will leave you wi' a head like a ball-bearing that's run over a lot of iron filings. Number four wi' . . .' I had to interrupt as I hadn't a clue what he was on about.

'I don't want to buy ball-bearings. I want a short-back-and-sides haircut to stop my wife throwing the hair that gets trapped in the plug hole after I've washed it at me,' I offered, by way of a feasible reason for being there.

He approached me growling to himself, 'Bloody typical! You try to offer them a service that's up to the minute and what thanks do you get? Bugger all.' Looking around him, he muttered, 'Where the hell did I put they scissors. Oh! There they are.' Lifting the scissors from out of a still warm mug of tea, he explained that he'd mislaid the teaspoon. As he wiped the hot tea off the scissors on to the coat – almost missing the aforementioned earwax – he informed me he had given up sugar for health reasons. 'You never know what's in the stuff you're eating these days.'

When he had finished, he placed a mirror at the back of my head. 'Alright?' he asked threateningly.

Scanning the mirror, I said if he could just put some Elastoplast on the various gouts of blood where the scissors had dug into my head, that would be fine.

'Nae bother! It's lucky that they scissors are blunt, they might have done some serious damage if they'd been sharp. Are you alright? You're looking a bit peely wally.'

I said I'd be fine eventually but, 'I wonder,' I asked. 'Could I sit down for ten minutes or so? I do feel a wee bit tired out.'

'It's maybe the loss of blood that's taking its toll, you know. You just sit on that box of bandages over by the front door till you feel alright.'

Thanking him for his generosity of spirit, I sank on to the bandage box and took in some air from the draught that was blowing in from the outside door.

'Can I get you anything, Minister? A wee drink o' this tea?' he asked.

'No thanks, Robert,' I replied. '. . . Well, maybe I could have a wee read of your paper?'

'There you go,' he said, passing the paper over. Pointing to a naked young lady's breasts, he remarked, 'Look at that, you could hang a wet duffel coat on her nipples.'

E VENTS HAVE TAKEN a new and terrible twist. I feel that I must ~~kronicel.chornicicle~~ write down these events accurately or I could be, as they say in the law courts, *in right soapy bubble.*

I was in the bathroom and had just finished wiping most of the blood away from the back of my neck after my visit to R. Sinparsley's hair emporium (thank God I didn't have a shave) when I heard from downstairs a shriek. It seemed to emanate from the very bowels of some unearthly creature that had not been cast from the Creator's mould.

'Have you hurt yourself, darling?' I shouted down.

I could sense trouble brewing like a dark cloud when her reply came. *'You! Down here! Now!'* she requested, rather forcibly it has to be admitted.

Wrapping a couple of sheets of toilet paper round my neck to keep the blood from staining my collar, I made my way downstairs.

'Where are you, pudding?' I asked needlessly as I stood in the doorway. I could hear her heavy breathing advancing from the living-room as if it had actual form. It seemed to roll from the living-room door through the hallway, where it crept up my legs, over my body and into my ears. It was heavy with menace and foreboding.

'Hello, pet,' I announced with a note in my voice that I forlornly hoped would assuage the almost certain hard time coming my way. 'Anything wrong?' I left the door open – in case.

She fixed me with a look that could have stripped varnish and handed me a letter. Her eyes bored into me as she said, *'Read this. Then explain.'*

My first thought was that she had found the letter from the Synod, and I was already trying to form an excuse for the poor attendances at church which would not leave me looking like a numpty. However, one glance at the format of the letter and

I could see that it was not the missive I dreaded. My spirits lifted.

'Well, let's have a look at it then,' I replied with a sense of confidence I had not felt a moment ago. 'Looks like a bill of some kind,' I advised, starting to read.

'"*The enclosed account is now overdue and prompt payment is requested or we will come round and give you a doing.*"'

I stared puzzledly at the invoice, and then my hands started to tremble as I read the header with the firm's name typed in bold lettering:

Erica's Erotic Massage Parlour

Featuring Norma – the Nympho's Nympho
& Gordon – the Man with the Golden Gonads
A discrete service for members of the clergy

To: Rev. I. M. Jolly
     The Manse
     Ruchgeddie
     Glasgow

To servicing the above.	
10 bondage sessions @ £20.00 :	£ 200.00
Supplying horny old squire and innocent young milkmaid outfits :	£ 100.00
One steamy sex session (straight) at £1 a minute :	£ 0.50
Total due :	£ 300.50

Thank you and come again

Erica

'No wonder you're shaking like a leaf,' Ephesia's voice cut through my horrified brain. 'You disgusting old pile of poo. How could you stoop so low? What's a gonad and why is it golden? Who's Erica? Where did you get 300 quid?' Her questions seemed to bounce like bullets inside my head.

'I've no idea,' I answered, skilfully dodging her head butt and running behind the settee. 'I've never heard of Erica, however I do know that a gonad is not usually golden unless you're David Beckham.' I hoped this information would make her pause for thought – in vain, I realised, as she threw the settee at me, thus removing my last line of defence. 'Let's calm down and try and reason this out between us,' I offered, backing round the room, trying the while to gauge where I was in relation to the door and safety. Her leg muscles grew taut and her ears flattened, a tell-tale giveaway that she was about to pounce. I had to escape quickly or I was dead meat.

I could see her gathering herself ready to spring. As she leapt across the room my hand had found the door handle. Thanking God I had had the foresight to leave the door open, I dodged through it and slammed it with a jarring sound against the frame. The door shook – so did the entire manse really – as Ephesia's bulk battered against it and I knew instinctively that the door would not hold out long. Fleeing down the hallway, I reached the outside and safety. I could still hear her cries of *'Filthy fornicating *******! I'll get you!'* I made a mental note to tell her about her language when – or if – we made up.

As I hurried down the road I could not for the life of me think what was going on.

Certainly my present of a Brillo Pad was not going to win her over, so the next best thing would be to find out what the invoice was all about and resolve the obvious case of mistaken identity to Ephesia's satisfaction. Picking the invoice out of my pocket, I read it again. On the back of it was an address. I had to go there and find out what this was all about.

I arrived at Erica's just as dusk was settling in. I obviously did not want to be recognised so this suited me down to the ground. A buzzer sounded as I closed the door hurriedly behind me. Seated under a pink, plastic portico behind a corn-coloured counter was a large lady dressed in a lilac see-through goonie.

'Are yez here to return the Presbyterian minister's outfit? You've made a right mess o' it, so yez have. I'll need to charge you for the dry cleanin', so I will,' she said in a voice that had smoked a million cigarettes.

'Eh, no. Actually I *am* a Presbyterian minister,' I said, not being able to take my eyes off the fact she had only her brassiere and underpants on underneath the goonie.

'Ah! You've heard aboot the discount deal for deacons,' she said alliteratively. 'Right, let's get your particulars down.'

My hands instinctively grasped my trousers and I held them in a grip of iron. 'You're no' taking *anything* of mine down,' I said in a voice that I hoped sounded authoritative.

She looked at me as if I were an oddity. 'What's your name?'

'The Rev. I. M. Jolly,' I said. 'And I . . .'

She stopped me with a dismissive wave. 'Oh! You're still in character! OK. Address? Don't tell me! The Manse, is it?' She giggled with more than a hint of irony. 'It'll be beautiful, eh! How big is it?'

Believing that truth is always the best option, I replied, 'It's not that big. I've just got a semi at the moment.'

'Well, don't you worry, I've got just the lassie to sort that out for you. Haw! Millicent?' she shouted over her left shoulder. 'When you've finished wi' Easy Rider, there's wan oot here wi' a semi.'

From a room in the dimly lit corridor behind the counter I heard a rather breathless female voice shout back, '*Aye, I'll be oot in a minute, Conceptua. Come oan, you. Hurry up,*' her voice urged some unseen companion.

'She'll no' be long,' said Conceptua in a calming way.

She leaned towards me, her bobble-abouts becoming more prominent the further she leaned. 'How would you like to pay?'

'That's what I've come here for,' I protested, closing my eyes. 'I've received a bill from you and I can swear on a stack of Bibles that I've never been near here in my life – up to now, that is.'

'Show me it,' she seemed to sigh seductively.

'I will not show you it! I'm a married minister.'

'I'm talking about the bill, show me the bill,' she said, wearily this time. I passed over the document in question. As she studied it I could hear Millicent's voice permeate from the room in the corridor. *'COME OAN YOU.* Bloody Viagra, it's ruining this business, so it is.'

Conceptua shook her head. 'This did not come from here. I've never seen this before. Somebody's winding you up, so they are. Did your wife see this?' I nodded disconsolately. 'Oh dear! That's no' funny. I feel heart sorry for you, Reverend Jolly.' I was grateful for her consoling words and I was also reminded that Mary Magdalene had been a woman of easy virtue and yet she had seen the error of her ways. Perhaps Conceptua's brush with a man of God had changed her also. She touched my arm gently as my head hung low. 'Still,' she whispered, 'now that you're here, you might as well be hung for a sheep as a lamb, eh? *Millicent! Are yez no' nearly done in there?'*

'*Naw! He's a wee swine this one, so he is,*' Millicent's reply came back. Not, I fear, unexpectedly.

Then a brainwave hit me, a way out. 'I wonder,' I asked. 'Could you give me a note saying that you've never seen me before?'

'Is it to show your wife?' Conceptua asked knowingly. I nodded. 'So you think a note from the madam of a massage parlour is going to swing the scales of justice your way, do you?'

I could see she had me figured for a right ninny. 'Not quite,' I replied. 'However, if you were to write a note saying that I did not come here for massages but that you were a grocery shop and I had come in for the *messages* then that might do it, eh?'

'*Haw, Millicent! I'll come in and gie you a hand wi' him,*' was the only reply I received to my suggestion.

Before I left I took a genuine invoice home to show Ephesia, and I'm glad to say that my dear wife accepted it as proof someone had indeed framed me, as they say in detective stories. She said she knew I was innocent because – how did she put it? 'Even if you paid for it, nobody would have you.' Still, it has left me wondering who could have done such a terrible thing to me. It could possibly have even resulted in Ephesia leaving me. I have resolved to track the one responsible down and urge them not to give up.

THIS MORNING I was christening again. It was a lovely day, clear with a frost that was now almost gone. The heat of the spring sun was bathing the scene in a warm, golden glow. The mother was an absolute picture. She was simply dressed in a pinkish two-piece suit which complemented the absolutely charming snow-white christening robe that draped round her shoulder, over her arms and cradled her little baby lovingly.

Not wanting to disturb her at such a tender moment, I turned to the girl next to her whom I took to be maybe the sister. 'And where is Baby's daddy, out working today?' I asked by way of an icebreaker.

Glaring at me she replied, 'The bastard's no' here, he slung his hook last night. Pig that he is, I hope he roasts in Hell.' She strafed me with a look that took in all points from my shoes to the top of my head. 'Could you fix that for us?' she enquired.

I was totally mystified by her question, not to mention terrified by her stare. 'What do you mean?' I replied, my voice wavering. 'Have you no' been listening to a word I've said?' she said. 'I said that I hope he roasts in Hell. And I'm asking if you can fix that for us?'

I was taken aback and stammered out, 'Eh! I'm afraid not.'

Again she looked at me as if I was something you would wipe off your shoe. 'Bloody men. Yez all stick together, don't yez. Call yourself a man of God? And you'll no' even try to get that poor wee innocent soul's bastard faither roasted in Hell. You're a disgrace to your collar.'

I reeled back from the onslaught then, recovering my composure, I offered, 'I could always have a word with the . . .' her eyes widened, 'illegitimate father,' I added hastily. 'And maybe get him to return and face up to his responsibilities?'

'You listen to me, Reverend Whatever-your-name-is. That pig is no' needed, right! And he's certainly no' wanted. So unless you can put a curse or somethin' on him, just christen this wee soul and be done wi' it.'

At that point the mother let out a yell. 'Ya wee besom, you, chuck that!' she called out with a rather nasally whine. This was due to the baby having grabbed one of the many metal rings the mother had pierced her left nostril with. 'Chuck it, Britney. You'll bleed my nose and get it all over my mammy's suit. You alright, Virago?' she whined to the Amazon standing next to me.

'Aye,' replied her aptly named friend. 'Face-and-a-half here is just being awkward, Madonna.'

I thought it was about time I stood up for myself, so I rounded on this female Gargantua and . . . apologised for getting her angry. I tried once more to explain that I was only seeking to bring the baby's parents together again, for the good of all concerned.

'I'm fed up telling you that he's neither wanted nor needed. Fortunately, her and I fancy one another, so we'll be a single-sex family, except there'll be three o' us, but all the same sex. In fact, we were gonnae ask you to marry us, but you've blown it noo.'

'I can't marry two women,' I blurted out. 'I've already married one and that has been a big enough shock to my system. The Bible tells us, "And woman shall not lie with woman",' I quoted wrongly.

Virago almost blew the cassock off me. 'It's no' us that are lying, it's that wee soul's bastard faither that was lying when he told my pal he was injured playin' rugby and couldnae have children, the lying bastard that he is.'

'Please keep your language respectable. You are in a church, if you remember,' I protested.

'Do you want to do this christening or do you no'?' spat out Virago. 'Because we're brassed off with your attitude, and I think I speak for Madonna when I say that.' She looked over to her friend – or should I say 'intended'.

Madonna nodded in acquiescence. 'Aye! You can speak for me, Virago. And I think I can speak for Britney.'

'You can't speak for a – how old is Britney?' I enquired.

'Six weeks,' Madonna volunteered.

'– Six-week-old child,' I continued. 'It has no mind of its own.'

Virago made a dive for me and screamed, 'Noo he's calling Britney brainless. I'm gonnae hook him.' She let loose with her right fist which, had I not had previous experience of evasive measures with Ephesia (no mean pugilist herself) might have landed on my jaw. I shaped as if to dodge left and then enlisted a shuffle that Prince Nasseem would have been proud of.

'Stand still till I belt you,' Virago howled as I ghosted off to the right. I taunted her, bobbing and weaving, with my hands at my side as I had once seen Muhammad Ali do in a fight.

'What's my name?' I called to her. Feinting in and out of her wild swings I was now in full Ali mode. As I danced around her I chanted mockingly, '"I float like a butterfly. I sting like a bee. Now what's my name? It's the Reverend Jollee." What's my name? What's my name?' I sung out. Virago had one last wild swing then collapsed at the side of the font. I felt a bit sorry for her; she was good, but not in Ephesia's class.

'You're a total basket case,' was the best she could come up with. She was beaten and she knew it.

Madonna stared down at her and with a hint of sadness in her voice said, 'I thought you could have taken *him* on. Come on, Britney, we'll go up to my mammy's.' She sloped wearily out of the church.

Virago trudged after her. Trying to regain her pride, she cajoled, 'I could have clouted him if he'd just stood still. Honest, I could have.' But there was no real conviction in her voice.

I was sorry that the baby had not been christened, but in another way I was relieved that I did not have to inflict the name 'Britney' on her. With a name like that she would never get anywhere.

I've often been asked what the 'I' and 'M' stand for in my name. I've never said, of course. My mother told me that I should have been called 'Ian Montgomery' Jolly. However, when they took me to get christened father was in a terrible hurry to go to a football match. Apparently the minister who performed the christening was a very nervous individual and suffered from a slight stammer when under stress. As he started to say, 'I christen you Ian . . . Ehhhh – Mont– . . . Mont– . . . Ehh . . .'

'Hurry up,' said my father.

'I, ehhh . . . emmmm . . .' continued the minister nervously.

'You better no' make me late,' said Daddy unhelpfully.

The minister was now even more nervous and tried to begin at the beginning.

'I – . . . I – . . . kkkk chri—ehhh, emmm.'

Father apparently was now beside himself with pent-up frustration. 'For God's sake, will you get a move on or I'll report you.'

The poor pastor was now a wreck. 'I – em – I – em – I – em –'

Father exploded. 'Right, I'm going to miss the match. Ceremony's finished, that'll do him. I'm away, come on Mother, and don't forget to take I. M. with you.'

I think maybe I'm a bit unlucky when it comes to christenings. I also think I might have made an enemy in Virago, and God alone knows I don't need any more of them.

THERE'S SOMETHING WEIRD going on in my life at the moment, something which I'm finding very difficult to figure out. It's getting so bad that I'm starting to dread opening the mail in the morning (I speak of the postal mail, not the newspaper *Mail*). First there was the bombshell from the Synod, then an invoice from Erica's – which is still a mystery as to why it was sent to me – and then this morning I received, well, let me recount exactly the events as they unfolded.

I had taken a long time to get to sleep last night due to the fact that Ranald was in the back garden practising on his trumpet. I told him it was 11.30 at night and he was annoying everyone. To be fair to Ranald, he apologised straightaway, packed up the trumpet and started to assemble his drum kit. There is really no reasoning with him when he is in one of his moods, so it's best to let him be.

I got out the earplugs Ephesia had got me for Christmas, inserted them into the appropriate orifices and settled down for a quick flip through the Old Testament before retiring for the night. Normally Ephesia does not take kindly to Ranald's little night music, be it trumpet, drums or his particular favourite, the tympani. But this evening she was humming quietly to herself with what, if I didn't know better, resembled a smile playing at the corners of her mouth.

'Ranald's taking a long time to get started on his drums,' I remarked. My voice seemed unusually loud, almost booming, whereas Ephesia's reply seemed unusually quiet, almost soft. I realised, of course, that I had forgotten to take the earplugs out and said, 'Sorry, petal, I forgot to take my earplugs out. I was saying, Ranald's taking a long time to start on his drums. I couldn't make out what you said.'

Ephesia's voice was familiarly loud and harsh – indeed, extremely loud (she hadn't removed her earplugs either). 'He'll find it harder without these,' she bellowed, holding up a pair of drumsticks. I decided to take a gander out the window that looked on to the back lawn where Ranald had set up his kit, and was amused to see him scratching his head and searching around for his drumsticks. After a while he gave up looking and decided to make do and mend with banging the drums with his head instead of the sticks. Although this was still noisy and annoying, it did have the advantage for us of knowing that Ranald was perhaps doing permanent damage to himself. We celebrated by deciding to have a sherry each: a glass for me and the usual bottle for Ephesia.

Ephesia is fond of what she calls a 'refreshment'. In fact, she is so fond, I have sometimes seen her as refreshed as a newt. We were almost halfway through a small repast when there was a knock on the back door. It was Ranald to say that, much as he was reluctant to give us some peace, he was going to have to pack in the drumming due to the fact that the skins were covered in blood from the cuts on his head.

'How did you cut your head on a drum skin?' I asked.

'It wasn't the drum skin. It was the cymbals,' he rationalised. 'I'm bored now,' he said menacingly. 'I think I'll just go for a rake round the graveyard. Do you want to chum me?' Grave-spotting was one of Ranald's abiding passions. Indeed, he used to say that and headering hand-grenades were the only things that kept him sane.

I've always found it wise to go with, rather than against Ranald so I made the excuse that I'd overdosed on grave-spotting for the time being and, rather than jade my appetite, I would sacrifice a week's spotting lest I dampen my enthusiasm. He sympathised, gave me a parting kick in the groin and left singing, 'I talk to the trees. One day they'll put me away. I speak to the walls. One day they'll cut off my . . .' His voice faded as he turned the corner.

As I closed the back door the old grandfather clock in the hall registered 12 a.m. by chiming eleven times. I never did figure out how to change it for British Summer Time and back again in the winter, so we gave up trying to work out whether it was accurate or not and just got the binoculars out and looked at the neighbour's clock across the road.

I knew that the night could hold fresh terrors for me when I saw that Ephesia had emptied the sherry bottle and was now looking at me in a way that always sends shivers down my back, through my legs, round my feet, up past my knees, stomach, chest, face, head and down my back again. Opening a fresh bottle of sherry, she let down her hair, let out a belch and purred, 'Mummy doesn't have a headache tonight. So who's a lucky boy then?'

Lucky was shaking in his shoes as she kicked off her baffies and huskily announced, 'I'm just going to the bathroom for a shave.' I was absolutely *beside* myself. What worried me was in ten minutes I would be beside *Ephesia*. The only course open to me was to have, as we in the trade say, 'A word with the boss'. Quickly, I got down on my knees, clasped my hands in prayer and, in a voice barely above a whisper, I implored Him to rescue me.

'Dear God. Oh please! Please! Lift this burden from me . . .' (shortly I would mean this literally) '. . . let me faint or something – at a push, I'll even accept a mild stroke.' I could hear the rasp of a razor from the bathroom and the blood froze in my veins. 'I don't want to rush you, Lord, but if you are going to help you'll have to be quick. She's nearly finished shaving. I've hidden her aftershave so that should hold her up for a bit, but once she finds it I'm hung out to dry.'

I could hear her shouting, 'Where's the bloody aftershave? Have you been using my aftershave? Mummy may have to punish her wee boy if he's used it all,' she threatened coquettishly.

'*Help! Help!*' my mouth screamed silently and then – a glimmer of hope – I saw that she had left her glass of sherry behind. My brain raced feverishly as a way out began to hatch in my head. It bounced round and round, seeming to take form and then in a flash disappearing into the recesses of my mind, and then – oh joy of joys! – it reassembled and floated to the front of my consciousness and took root.

Grasping up the glass of sherry, I approached the bathroom door and knocked tentatively. 'Can I come in, pumpkin?'

Grabbing me by the bottom lip, she hauled me in. 'Where's the aftershave?' she asked, shaking me profusely.

'*Awahwawah uhuhwawah,*' I replied incoherently, as she was still holding me by the bottom lip.

'Oh, Mummy's sorry. Did Squidgie Widgie see Mummy's aftershave?' Squidgie Widgie nodded. 'Well, would Squidgie Widgie get it for Mummy?' she hiccuped. Squidgie freed himself from Mummy's grip and moved over to the toilet bowl where he deftly opened the top of the cistern and removed the aftershave in question from where he'd hidden it. Mummy was too pissed to notice Squidgie do this. Squidgie dried the bottle on the back of his shirt and handed it to Mummy. While Mummy was splashing herself with Old Spice, Squidgie edged over to the medicine cabinet. Opening the door of the cabinet Squidgie took a bottle of sleeping tablets from the second shelf and put six of them into the glass of sherry he was hiding behind his back. Squidgie then put another four pills in the glass, just to be on the safe side.

'Would Mummy like to finish her sherry before she and Squidgie go beddie byes?' said Squidgie, edging his way out the door and handing Mummy the glass. Ten minutes later Squidgie breathed a sigh of relief when he heard Mummy hit the floor with a dull thud and start snoring, as only Mummy could.

I slept fitfully through the night probably because I was subconsciously feeling guilty at having slipped Ephesia a Mickey Finn. (I wonder if Mr and Mrs Finn knew that their son Mickey

would one day be a household name?) I'd been having a
nightmare about a man trying to saw my legs off, which made
me wake up in a cold sweat. I was confused because my legs
felt sore but, although I could still hear this sod sawing, I could
not *see* him sawing. I couldn't even see the saw, although my
mind was seesawing with the confusion of the sawer not being
seen, but reason finally triumphed when I realised there was no
sawer to be sawed, the saw was the sound of my dear wife's
drug-induced comatosity aggravating her chronic adenoidal
condition, i.e. snoring. The end result was a noise louder than
a whale with a flatulence problem's bum could make.

A cup of tea and a slice of toast seemed a very good idea. I
threw my legs over the side of the blanket and embarked on my
regular exercise routine. Up, down, up, down, up, down, up,
down, up, down. Now the same with the right eyelid. Up,
down, up, down, up, down, up, down, up, down. I was starting
to feel better already.

Padding past Ephesia's bedroom (drugged or not, I was taking
no chances), I gathered up the mail and trundled through to the
kitchen. While I waited for the kettle to boil, I opened the
various garbage that passed for correspondence. I had again
been selected from a select few and would now be almost
certain to win half a million pounds if I would only return the
form entitling me to hundreds of books that I would never
read, for a ridiculously low subscription. *Rip, tear, into the bin.*
I had also been selected, blah, blah, blah, to be a privileged
customer of at least eight different credit cards. Entitling me to
spend all the money I don't have. *Rip, tear, into the bin.* According
to this next load of old codswallop, I'm mature enough to
appreciate that this new all-natural but miracle herbal concoction
will cure me of baldness, banish my rheumatism and make me
a raging stud (whatever that is). *Rip, tear, into the bin.* If I wasn't
so cheerful it would make me boak. I opened another one.

It has been reported to the Synod that you have been seen smoking substances which are unlawful. The Church frowns on these substances because they may make you happy when you've no right to be. The person who grassed you up (no pun intended) says they saw you smiling after inhaling deeply from a *very* long cigarette. You are by reputation one of our more miserable ministers. In light of this we are prepared to let you off with a warning. *This time.*

You were also reported by this civic-minded Christian for sniffing coke. However, we have overlooked this in light of the fact that coca cola is not on the banned list. We do suggest that you try drinking it though, considering you are synonymous with a nasal drip at least your nostrils won't get any wetter.

How are the attendances?

Niven Simmons

NIVEN SIMMONS
ASSISTANT TO WILSON SIMMONS BUT NO RELATION,
ALTHOUGH THE HANDWRITING IS VERY SIMILAR.

This, coupled with the massage parlour invoice, leads me to think someone is writing poison pen letters about me, but who? And, more importantly, why?

TODAY MY HOPES of enlarging my congregation were boosted by one. Admittedly it was old Mr Crabbit, who had turned up looking for the three quid that he thought (wrongly) I was going to give him, but nevertheless on paper it was statistically true that I had seen a fifty per cent increase in my flock. I gave him one of my especially warm 'nice to see you back at church' smiles. In response he merely took out his wallet, opened it, mouthed silently, 'You owe me', and held up three fingers.

I was tempted to start bargaining all over again. Fortunately, however, I realised in the nick of time that if I held up two fingers it might be misconstrued by the rest of the congregation. So I simply held up my hand with the tip of my thumb joining the tip of my index finger making a circle and gave him a salute. This he took to be me signalling OK. What I was actually signalling was, 'You're getting nothing.'

The gist of my sermon was from the Gospel according to Saint Matthew, and traces the sons of Abraham.

MATTHEW 1, VERSE 2

And Abraham begat Isaac, and Isaac begat Jacob, and Jacob said to Isaac, 'I am going away.' And Isaac said unto Jacob, 'What are you away for?' And Jacob said unto Isaac, 'I am away for biscuits.' And Isaac was pleased, for he liked wafer biscuits. And Jacob searched throughout the land for biscuits made from wafer.

But a terrible drought had lain waste to the land and there had been a run on double nougats. And wafers were as scarce as wise men in the Scottish Parliament.

And the milk from cows turned sour in the sun and formed roundels of cheese and cream. And Jacob fell upon them and in his hunger did feast on the cheese, as that was his favourite thing in the whole world.

And the cream dried and caked in the sun. And the Israelites wailed and turned against their God. But Jacob fell on his knees and gathered unto him the remains. And he said, 'I will take these cakes and form them into biscuits for my father Isaac.'

And Jacob travelled throughout and to the land of Nod, where he had a nice wee kip.

And Jacob being refreshed did come upon his father's house and amazement was on his mother's face. And his mother said to her cat, 'Amazement get off my face for my son Jacob is come home.'

And Jacob placed the biscuits of cream on the table. And the cat did play with the biscuits and did drop them on the ground and the biscuits did crack. And Jacob wept as he gathered the cracked biscuits of cream and laid them on the table. And Jacob ran from his father's house, for he had failed his father.

And Isaac the father of Jacob did see the table and he said unto his wife, 'What are these?' and his wife said, 'These are Jacob's Cream Crackers.' And Isaac did rejoice.

At this point old Crabbit stood up and shouted, 'I'm no sufferin' any more of this garbage. Even for three quid. It's no wonder that you're for the sack. The rumour is you're smoking grass noo. Grass is for mowin', no' smokin'. Keep your money.'

I was very concerned that the other two in the church would hear this and start making monetary demands of their own from me. Of course, I need not have worried on that score, they were good and faithful members of my little congregation. They were also sound asleep.

Waiting until old Crabbit was out of harm's way, I put the kettle on, made myself a cheese toastie and a cup of tea, and settled down for a read at the Sunday papers. They were full of tales of human misery, financial disasters and governmental cock-ups. It was all I could do to put them down. However, you can get too much of a good thing, and anyway it was time to wake up my congregation. Putting on my cassock (which is optional, but I like it), I let myself in by the side door. I could see that both of them were still out of it, so I started to sing at the top of my voice, 'Stand up, stand up for Jesus'. This did the trick and, after the initial confusion and cries of 'Where the hell are we?', they settled and joined in with the closing verses.

As I stood outside in the cold, they were full of praise when I bade them good afternoon.

'A wonderful sermon, Reverend Jolly,' said old Mrs Rishious.

'Thank you very much, Ava.' I turned to shake hands with Ava Rishious's friend, Miss Gostura, who was blowing her nose on my cassock. Rumoured to be of foreign extraction, she was a delightful lady who unfortunately suffered from very poor vision. 'And how are we today, Ann?' I enquired.

'Very well, vicar,' she replied, trying to stuff the hem of my cassock up her sleeve. She surveyed it with a grimace and shaking her head informed no one in particular, 'I must remember to wash this hanky, it's black, so it is.'

Ava Rishious whispered into my ear, 'Ann has written a wee poem for you, Reverend Jolly.'

'Is that so?' I enthused, removing my cassock from Miss Gostura's sleeve. 'Ava tells me you've written a wee poem for me, Ann.'

'That's right, Reverend Jolly. You've lost an awful lot of weight,' she said to the flagpole I was standing next to at the entrance to the Kirk.

'May I see your poem, Ann?'

Nodding shyly she searched in her bag. After a moment she handed over a bit of paper. 'I hope you like it?' she said to the flagpole.

Taking it from her I started to read. 'This is to inform you that your cold weather allowance is going up by fifteen pence.' Realising that a mistake had been made, we all had a right good laugh when I said quick as a flash, 'That's not the poem, is it?'

When we had all calmed down Ann Gostura finally placed the poem in my hand. It read:

Roses are red
Violets are orange
Blackbirds are yellow
And so are green finches.

'How very, very true,' said Ava loyally, but mistakenly.

'I want you to keep it,' Ann said to the flagpole.

As they walked away from me arm and arm into the gathering gloom I must admit I thought to myself, 'What a pair of plonkers.'

ANOTHER NIGHT OF INTERRUPTED SLEEP. I really can't carry on like this. Something is bound to snap. I decided to take an inventory of what was worrying me and see if I could put it all into perspective.

One. I was in danger of being discarded from the calling that I had felt pulled towards from my early childhood. When all my friends were out playing Cowboys and Indians, I was engrossed in the Old Testament, trying to interpret the ancient sayings and make them relevant to my school chums. I told them the story of Lot and how his wife was turned into a pillar of salt and how relevant it still was to us today, even as we played at Cowboys and Indians. But they only laughed at me and made me into a figure of fun. I found solace in the words of the Bible even then. Sodom, I thought. Mind you, we all laughed at wee Bobby Tarif because of the way he dressed. He dressed in a dress. I often wonder what became of wee Bobby.

My contemporaries also thought me a bit odd because of my dress sense. None of your 'What's the latest fashion?' for me. I wanted to look like a minister. Mother was always giving me a row for wearing my shirts back to front so it would look like a dog collar.

Father, of course, came up with the perfect compromise. 'If he wants a dog collar, give him one. I'll get you one, son,' he said, and he was true to his word. He even got me a leash to match and we had great fun. He would take me for walks and we would play fetch and chase cats. In fact, he played with me so much that by the time I was four years old, I could die for my country, heel, and give a paw when I wanted something to eat. Mother was especially proud when she realised that one look from my father and I would get down off the settee. She used to tell all her friends that Dad and I were so close it was almost telepathic.

There was, however a downside to all this innocent fun. It was impossible to go on holiday in the countryside as I developed a taste for worrying sheep. But on the bright side (which there always is), I did win Best in Show at the 'Bring your Pet to Church' day. Father didn't come with me. He said if I went by myself it would be killing two birds with the one stone and what was the point of having a dog and barking yourself anyway?

Of course, with the arrival of my brother Ranald I was inevitably neglected while my parents gave all their attention to the new baby. It was mother, though, who noticed that I was below par. She took me in her arms and examined me and informed father that my hair was matted and my nose was dry. Father, to his credit, went straight down to the corner shop and came back with a box of Bob Martins which restored the sheen to my hair and also made my nose wet again. Indeed, to this day my nose has never failed to be moist – surely a testament to the care that I received as a ~~pup~~ boy.

I digress, however, from my original intention to set out the things that I should be worried about. I suppose that an inability not to digress is something to worry about. I'll put that down as number two. What was the first one again? Oh dear, I can't remember. I suppose I'd better put that down as number three. Periodic loss of memory. As Genesis 9 reminds us: 'Noah was drunken and lay in his tent. And he was reprimanded for loitering with intent.' That's not an accurate quotation, of course, but it'll tide me over till I can think of one more apt. Now, where was I? There I go, digressing again. I'll really have to watch that one. That's a big worry. It's up there with the first one. Whatever that was. I've forgotten again.

That's periodic loss of memory, that is. Have I put that down already? Yes, of course I did – that was number three. Good, I'm back on track now.

Fourth worry. How do I boost my congregation in order to make the first worry go away and not worry me? I've tried talent contests to whet their appetite; no good. Then inadvertently the potential membership were led to believe that I had won the Lotto and might share it with them; that was no good either when the parasites/potential church members found out I was skint. I've even tried bribery with old Crabbit and that went belly up too.

Well, as far as I'm concerned ten out of ten for initiative. Of course, that won't count with those bloodsuckers in the Synod. I might just point out to them:

MATTHEW 18, VERSE 20

For where two or three are gathered together in my name, there am I in the midst of them.

I have two, what more do they want? It seems to have been good enough for the Saviour but not for the mighty Synod. I'm digressing again, albeit with justification. Still I am doing it and I must stop.

Nevertheless, I could also point out to them that ours is a religion founded on mercy and forgiveness. As Jesus said, 'The quality of mercy is not strained, but droppeth like a gentile Jew out of the frying pan into the fire.' Was that Jesus or was it Shakespeare? Or maybe it was my granny. Oh dear, I've managed to misquote, digress and forget all at the one time.

I forgot for a moment that someone seems to be sending me poison pen letters as well. There was the dreadful business of Erica's massage parlour. Ephesia may have forgiven but she never forgets. She has the memory of an elephant if not the texture – although I suspect that's only down to the two jars of mud-pack she plasters on each afternoon. She looks like a swamp with teeth.

I took her to a garden party once and her face won first prize for texture and the ability to hold manure. We were having a cup of tea at the side of the marquee when a young man and his girlfriend came round the corner. They only had eyes for each other and as he got down on one knee and gazed up at her, Ephesia said, 'I think he's going to propose, and he doesn't realise we're here. You'd better whistle and warn him.'

'What for?' was my doleful reply. 'Nobody warned me.'

There I go, digressing *again. Stop. Stop. Concentrate.* Emmm? Poison pen letters, that was it. Erica. Yes. And of course, there was the accusation of substances abuse sent to the Synod. I haven't replied to that letter from them yet. I have to choose my words carefully or I could be hoisted by my own lanyard. It may even be better to ignore them and play the whole thing as if I was treating it as a joke.

The doorbell rang. That's what to do, I confirmed to myself as I went to open the front door, laugh the whole thing off as two pranks in very poor taste.

I opened the door still smiling as I secretly congratulated myself on my plan of inaction. 'Yes. What can I do for you?' I said to the two men standing at the door.

'Reverend Jolly?' asked the taller of the two.

'That's me,' I replied.

'We've had an anonymous tip-off that you've been stealing lead off your own church roof,' he announced, showing me his detective's badge. The smaller of the two showed what I thought were remarkable reflexes when he caught me just as I plummeted to the floor in a dead faint.

I came to lying on the floor in a cold cell. My immediate thought was that my feet were bare. Why had my shoes been taken away?

A shaft of light shone through from a window set high enough on the far wall to make it impossible to reach, except by standing on a chair. I knew without looking there would not be one.

Trying to recollect my thoughts, I attempted to rise from my prone position. My brain spun round inside my head making me weak. The cell was spinning and my legs buckled under me. My breath came in short frantic gulps and I had to settle for squatting on all fours with my head resting on the cell wall.

The wall, cold on my forehead, was strangely soothing and

110

seemed to be the first tangible sense of something approaching reality that I could hang on to. I don't quite know how long I stayed in that position. It felt somehow comforting. Then I heard a noise. It seemed to be from inside the cell. It played around my head and I tried in my confusion to unravel the sound and make sense out of it. It was . . . scratching, that was it, scratching. My spirits began to revive. Could there be a companion? A fellow unfortunate who had through some cruel twist of fate been predestined to share his suffering with my own. Was he trying to scratch his way through the cell walls to the outside world? Would he take me with him? Why was I here? Questions flew back and forth and collided with unformed doubts that squashed and squeezed and converged into a quagmire of confusion.

The prospect of being able to converse and console was like manna from Heaven.

With a Herculean push, I raised myself on to my feet and staggered back slightly with the effort. The scratching stopped and a squeal of rage rang through the stagnant air of the cell. Something was under my right heel? I looked round, over my shoulder and down to my feet. Every nerve in my body screeched out with the terrible sight that my eyes had affixed themselves to. Under my heel was a tail. It was long and powerful and thrashing around in a frenzy of fear and fury. At the end of it was an enormous dark *rat*.

It jumped on to my foot. Trying to free itself, it clung to my trousers, its claws penetrating the cloth and making my skin crawl as they made contact. Its eyes locked on to mine and, with a glare of pure hatred, it began to strain and stretch its taut body, trying to release its tail from under my foot. I froze with the horror of it and then my sanity snapped. A furrow appeared along the length of its spine, and from the point that the tail joined its body it ripped along its back up through the neck and tore itself free. The rat's tail was still trapped under my heel but its body was now hurtling upwards towards my gaping mouth. My hands tried to protect my face. Too late, its teeth were already starting their deadly work and I could feel its claws on my cheeks.

I fought as valiantly as I could and was aware that I was beginning to gain the upper hand when the rat said, 'Are you alright, Reverend Jolly, you've had a wee turn.'

The rat was slapping me gently on the cheeks and trying to force a cup of warm, sweet tea between my lips.

'Away you go, you dirty rat,' I rasped through clenched teeth.

'Now, now, Reverend Jolly,' said the rat. 'There's no need for abusive language. I was only doing what I'm paid to do.'

Another, smaller rat took out a notebook, put on a pair of rimless spectacles and sat on *my* chair. I felt justified in saying to him, 'That's my chair you're sitting on, you wee rat.'

The rat with the spectacles shook his head, and the one trying to give me a cup of tea said, 'I must warn you that anything you say might be taken personally and could result in a severe kick in the goolies, reverend or no' reverend. So if I were you, I'd watch it.'

I started to make sense of what was shaping up to be a nightmare. 'You're the police, aren't you?'

They nodded.

'What was it you wanted again? I seem to have forgotten. I was being attacked by a rat and it's went right out my head. Not the rat. What you were wantin' has gone out of my head.'

The tall policeman looked at me strangely as if I wasn't right in the head, which I resented. 'Did you give me a strange look?' I said challengingly.

'You've got a strange look alright, but I never gave you it,' he replied confidently as his partner nodded in agreement.

He took a pencil from his top pocket and tapped it against his bottom lip and then started to chew on it. 'We received an anonymous letter accusing you of stealing the lead off of your own church roof. And we would like to know what you have to say to that. For what it's worth, we don't believe you have, but it's something that we must follow through. So where have you stashed the lead?' I gasped out loud. 'Sorry! I meant, what do you have to say to the accusation?'

Fixing him with a stare of righteous indignation I replied, 'Not guilty! Do I look like the sort of person who would steal lead from the roof of a Church of Scotland kirk?'

'No,' said the tall policeman with a wry smile. He removed his pencil from his mouth, 'I don't believe you do.'

'I'm not tho thure,' said Specky. 'Hith eyebrowth are a bit clothe together and that'th uthually a thure thign that criminal tendenthieth are prethent in an accuthed.'

'He's right enough there, Reverend,' said Lanky, chewing thoughtfully on his bottom lip then howling with pain because he forgot he'd removed the pencil. Taking a hanky from his top pocket, he attempted to stem the flow of blood which – I'm ashamed to say – the sight of, filled me with delight and a renewed sense that justice had just been seen to be done. 'I think we'd better go and take a look at that roof. Just for the record. Would you like a lift in the squad car? Or would you rather we just frog-marched you down to the church so fast that your feet don't touch the ground? It's entirely up to you.'

'I hope he goeth for the frog-march. I think we look pure galluth when we have to do that,' four-eyes interjected with a smirk that made you just want to smack him till the fillings in his teeth fell out.

I must confess I was beginning to feel a bit annoyed with both of them, but Specky was really not going to be in my prayers tonight. 'I'm innocent of all charges, and demand to see a lawyer who will get me off scot-free and win me a very substantial libel suit for defamation of character and false arrest. And further more,' I added, 'notice that I said "arrest" and not "arretht", which is more than you can do, Specky!'

Specky began to go quite purple with rage. 'I can tho thay "arretht",' he said, falling into my trap.

'No! You can not,' I teased.

'Yeth I can tho.' He was beginning to get ever so slightly hysterical. 'Thure I can thay "arretht"?' he asked his partner in crime, who shrugged a bit embarrassedly as he stared firmly at the floor beneath his feet. 'Well tell him!' Four-eyes was now beginning to sense he was standing on shifting sands, a phrase which I was not going to let go to waste.

'I think you're standing on shifting sands with this,' I goaded.

'I am not thtanding on thyifting thands. You can't thay that.' He was now beginning to stamp his feet.

'No. You've got it wrong there. I can say "shifting sands", it's you who can't say "shifting sands",' I went on relentlessly.

Four-eyes was by now a quivering mass of uncontrollability. 'Tell him to thtop,' he screeched.

Lanky placed his hand on my shoulder and said, 'I think this has gone far enough, don't you?'

I was non-committal in my reply. 'If he says so. Do you say so?' I addressed my question with a thin veneer of innocence to Specky, who was by now beginning to feel his tongue was like a nervous anaconda writhing around between his teeth.

'Yeth! Yeth! I thay tho – thatithfied?'

I really was enjoying myself now. 'Would you say you were susceptible to scathing and cynical scepticism?' I inquired.

'Don't go there,' interrupted Lanky quickly. He turned to me. 'From what I can gather, you say you know nothing about this allegation. Do you have any idea who the alligator might be?'

Specky was sobbing in a corner of the room so I decided enough was enough. I am, after all, a man of God and believe that mercy and forgiveness are the most precious gifts we have to grant our fellows – even this snivelling little toady bubbling in the corner.

'No. I have dedicated my life to helping others. There is not a soul in the whole wide world that I have ever borne malice to or harmed in any way. I can't think of anyone who would wish me ill.'

'I with you were ill. I with you were *dead*,' sobbed Specky.

Lanky flashed him a look that spoke volumes. 'I think we'll go down to the kirk and have a look for ourselves, get this mess sorted out once and for all. What do you say, Reverend?'

'Yes that will be fine,' I agreed. 'If it's not too cheeky, could I ask your name, detective?'

'Yes. Of course. I am Detective Inspector Sergeant and this is Constable Poalis, who is in the plain-clothes division. Shall we go then?'

While I locked up, the two policemen were standing at the side of their car waiting for me to join them. Constable Poalis, who had taken his coat off and was now in uniform, was at the front obviously going to drive. As I walked towards them Detective Inspector Sergeant opened the rear door and beckoned me into the back seat. I slid in and, with a gesture that was inviting me to move over, he joined me in the back seat and shut the car door. Poalis sat himself down behind the wheel, closed the door and activated the central locking system. I could see his eyes glaring at me from the rear-view mirror as he started the engine up. Or didn't, as it turned out. The only sound that came from the engine was a whine. He tried again and was met with the same result – whine, whine, whine.

'Sounds like somebody I know,' I said, trying to add a touch of humour to the situation. Unfortunately, Poalis took this to be a reference to his breakdown in the big room of the manse and started to cry again.

Sergeant undid his seat-belt and said, 'It sounds like the starter motor has jammed. I'm afraid we'll have to walk.'

Poalis got out of the car and as I stood up he shut the car door behind me. Pinning my arms to my sides he cried out in triumph, 'Frog-march, thir?'

'Aye. Frog-march it is, Constable Poalis,' said Detective Inspector Sergeant, grabbing me by the left arm. Constable Poalis held on to my right arm as he locked the doors. Amazingly my feet were not touching the ground.

As I was manhandled down to the kirk, I kept protesting my innocence. 'I am a man of the cloth, I'll write to my MSP, I'll write to the Moderator of the Church of Scotland.' Mentally, I made a note not to bother writing to my MSP as I'd never met anyone who knew where or even who the MSP was. I made another mental note not to write to the Moderator either, seeing as how I was not exactly flavour of the month at CoS GHQ (that's short for Church of Scotland General Headquarters – it just saves me writing it out in full, which I've just done, I suppose). 'I'm not without friends, you know,' I threatened.

'Oh, thut up,' said you know who as we rounded the corner and passed old Mr Crabbit's garden. He was polishing the leaves on his privet hedge with a Mr Sheen aerosol as we passed. Without looking round he said, 'Good – you've arrested him at last. Long overdue, if you ask me. He's got away wi' murder for years. Has he tried to bribe you yet? You'll no' get your money off him so be warned.'

Poalis's eyes sparkled. 'Murder, eh?' he whispered into my ear. Then speaking up he added. 'I think we might jutht have opened up a hornet'th netht here, Detective Inthpector.'

Detective Inspector Sergeant nodded sagely. 'Aye, with a bit of luck he might even turn out be one of them serial killers. There might be bodies everywhere.'

'Fingerth crothed,' Poalis lisped irritatingly.

Mr Majid was replacing the iron grill on the front of his shop window. Due to the high standard of vandalism we had, this was a weekly task but he quite enjoyed it. 'It gets me out of the shop,' he told people. The constabulary stopped to have a word with him.

'Is this not Tuesday?' enquired Sergeant. Mr Majid nodded. 'But surely you always get broken into on a Monday?'

Mr Majid nodded again. 'Monday was a bank holiday,' he offered by way of an explanation.

The DI smiled. 'Silly me, of course it was. Did you catch a glimpse of them?'

Mr Majid signalled yes with a nod as he struggled to put the grill on the metal supports at the side of the window.

'Neighbourhood Watch again, eh?' said the DI ruefully. 'Oh well, back to work I suppose.' Still in frog-marching mode, my feet dragged on the pavement as I was pulled along.

As he slid the grill on to its anchor points, Mr Majid shouted out after us, 'I can take a hint. I'll contribute to the police ball next time.'

By this time we had almost reached R. Sinparsley's hair umporium. The door opened and I could see Robert trying to keep it ajar with one leg, while gingerly holding a basin of blood in his hands. Having completed this manoeuvre, he was emptying the blood down the drain as we drew level. The ever-alert constabulary were motivated to open enquiries.

'That's an awful lot of blood you're emptying down the drain, Robert,' said Sergeant suspiciously.

'Aye, it's Tuesday. Two for the price of one,' explained Robert. 'It's no' all blood anyway. It's blood mixed wi' hair, skin and a wee drop water to make it flow doon the drain quicker. Has he been tea leafing again?' he continued, glancing towards me.

'We're not thure yet. We're thtill in an enquiry thituathion,' said Poalis grandly.

'Well. I'm sure he half-inched a *Daily Record* and a *Sun* oot of here the other day. I've no concrete proof, mind you. Nothing that would stand up in a court of law. But it was him, I know it was him definitely. But as I say, I've no proof. But I'm willing to perjure myself in court if it would get him and his like off our streets. I'm away up to Majids to stock up on Elastoplasts. I always go through a stack on a Tuesday,' he said walking away, his shoes squelching as he left a trail of bloodstained footprints behind him.

'We could do with a few more like him in the community, eh Poalis?' said Sergeant.

'I thyould thay tho, Thergeant,' Poalis acquiesced in his vocally-challenged way. Both of them were now looking at me as if I had just crawled out from beneath a stone or was a community councillor. I felt very low indeed. I now wished that we could get to the church as soon as possible before any more circumstantial evidence mounted up. No such luck.

A voice rang out from the other side of the road. It was the woman whose child I had dropped into the font. 'Good, you've got him. He tried to drown my baby, you know, and then he threw the wean at my husband. I'm still attending the doctor wi' my nerves, thanks to him.' She paused a while to light up a cigarette. 'And another thing as well. My husband's had to go off work and on the social due to post-traumatic syndrome because of that animal.' She took a long drag at her cigarette. 'And I'll tell yez something else. If yez were to concentrate on lifting the likes of him instead of hounding innocent local vandals and house-breakers and drug pushers who, by the way, are keeping the local economy going, yez would maybe be thought a lot better of in the community. My mother brought me up to try and see the good in everybody, but that's a pure animal that. His poor wife must be in a hell of a state wi' him, and by the way she's not been seen for a while noo.' She poured herself a cup of coffee from a flask and sat down on one of those collapsible three-legged stools which are on sale in garden shops. 'Noo! I'm not suggesting he's done her in or anything, but I wouldn't put it past him, you know. Have you seen the price of a bag of sugar up in that Majid's? Scandalous, so it is.' She drew on her cigarette and took a sip at her coffee, then made a face. 'No' enough sugar. You know my sister's man

Frankie?' As Sergeant shook his head with impatience, wanting to be on his way, she continued. 'You do so. Yez have lifted him many a time, you must remember him! Yez are always liftin' him. Last Wednesday it was drunk and disorderly – that was an overnight; then on the Thursday, drunk in charge of a stolen vehicle – his lawyer got him oot on bail wi' that. I forget what Friday was noo, eh, oh aye, drunk and exposing himself. He's a right laugh, so he is. You must know him. He stands at the corner of the clinic pushing drugs every Saturday mornin' before he goes to the football.'

Sergeant shook his head again. 'I'm afraid not. We get a lot of petty crime round here and they all tend to blend in after a while. But we think this one here,' he gave me an almost affectionate hug, 'might just lift us out of the hum-drum and on to the front pages.'

'Right enough,' she agreed. 'He looks as if he's been hidin' something dark inside. Is it my imagination or are his eyebrows no' a wee bit too close thigether for comfort?'

'Thatth what I thaid,' announced Specky triumphantly.

At this, another passer-by shouted to the sole representative of the district's café society: 'Virginia, your Frankie's just set fire to himself again. He's a bloody laugh, isn't he?'

'Tell me aboot it,' said Virginia, waving her hand in a gesture of mock despair.

Putting the flask away, she stubbed out her cigarette and as she folded up her stool she said with the air of a woman whose patience was inexhaustible. 'I'd better away and help put him oot. Nice to talk to yez, though, and I'm glad to see yez are getting your priorities right,' she added, giving me a withering glance as she walked off to attend to her incendiaric brother-in-law.

'Right, let's get to the scene of the crime and wrap this one up,' grunted Sergeant as he and Poalis put me back into frog-march mode. 'The sooner you're in custody and locked up with the key thrown away, the safer we'll all feel.'

'I would like to point out that in this country one is innocent until proven guilty,' I protested.

'Really,' sneered Sergeant. 'Well, I'd like to point out that I have been in the force for twenty odd years . . .' (very *odd*, I thought to myself) '. . . and after a time you develop a nose for the really bad cases. And let me tell you, Reverend, that right now I'm smelling really bad.'

'I'm thmelling ath well,' crowed Specky as we turned into the churchyard gates.

Sergeant stood with one hand gripping me and the other shading his eyes from the watery sun, as he looked up towards the roof of the kirk.

'I think there may be a few slates loose,' I ventured.

'Can't see any,' said Sergeant.

'I wasn't referring to the roof,' I explained.

'I'm going to enjoy putting you behind bars, you know that? I'm also going to enjoy duffing you up when you resist arrest,' smiled Sergeant.

'I won't resist arrest then,' I countered.

'Oh yes you will,' he said with an air of finality that stated the matter was no longer up for debate.

Unlocking the door, we entered the kirk and after a summary survey of the geography of the church he said, 'Right. Let's get into the loft. You lead and we'll follow.'

'And no funny bithneth,' added Specky irritatingly.

With the inspector and Poalis in close attendance behind me, I made my way up the winding stairs that led to the loft. A silent prayer that my innocence would be established was on my lips. Secretly, I feared that whoever the fiend was who had been hounding me with these poison pen letters may have been so vengeful that they actually could have stolen lead from the roof.

My heart was pounding as we entered the loft space.

120

Handcuffing me to Specky, Sergeant took out a torch and, with a meaningful look into my eyes, he said menacingly, 'Prepare to resist arrest, parson. Watch him closely, Poalis.'

Gingerly, he stepped along the joists, scanning the roof with his torch. There was no sound except for the creaking of the joists as Sergeant slowly and carefully examined each section with his torch. Making careful and methodical sweeps of light along each section of the roof, the action reminded me of those prisoner-of-war pictures where the spotlights scanned the German concentration camps looking for allied prisoners trying to escape from their clutches so they could rejoin their units and end the hell that was war. I always liked the bit where the hero would –

Oh no, I'm digressing again. How could I digress at a moment like this? I must get a firm hold on that side of my thinking or –

My thoughts were interrupted. 'Ah! What's this, then?' Sergeant shouted out from far away down the loft space. My breath stopped as my worst fears leapt to the front of my brain with a foreboding certainty that I could almost taste.

I heard Specky whisper into my ear, 'I'm going to thump you thtupid.'

Despite the gloom in the loft, my eyes could dimly make out Specky drawing out his baton from its resting place.

'Thith ith going to hurt you a lot more than it'th going to hurt me,' he giggled as he called out, 'Thyall I thtart without you, thir, thoften him up for you a bit?'

Poalis swung his baton and struck out at my unprotected head. The impending blow missed due to the fact that luckily, at that precise moment, my legs buckled from under me causing the baton to swish narrowly but harmlessly over me. It was brought to a sudden and jarring halt as it slammed into a roof strut causing Specky to howl in pain as his arm went into spasm.

'That'th thore,' he squealed.

121

'What the hell's going on?' said Sergeant, his torch beam growing larger as it snaked along the floor joists towards where I was cowering in the foetal position, my free arm shielding my head protectively.

'It'th hith fault. I tried to thmack him one on the head, he ducked and made me mith and I hurt my arm,' was the rational explanation that Specky offered in his defence.

Detective Inspector Sergeant's voice had a stern and commanding ring to it as he replied, 'Constable Poalis, I'm going to pretend I never heard that. That is not the way responsible police officers go about their business. We do not beat suspects about the head with batons. I'll remind you that in the police force we have a code of conduct to honour. In the future I will expect you to remember that and beat them about the legs and body where we can blame it on a fall. Got that?'

'Thorry, thir,' said Specky sheepishly. 'Did you find the thpot where he had thtripped off the lead?' he mumbled, rubbing at his arm. This was a question that interested me also. I tried to glean some clue as to the answer that could map out my future as a curate or a convict.

'This was pinned to a roof strut,' Sergeant said with a note of intrigue in his voice as he waved what looked like a sheet of cheap toilet paper. 'As for the lead stripping,' he turned his gaze firmly on to me, 'unfortunately there does not seem to be any evidence to support that allegation.' His voice contained more than a hint of disappointment, and I couldn't help but get the feeling that he held me responsible for not being guilty. He turned to Poalis. 'Let's get out of here.'

As we entered the church proper, I could feel the weight of the ordeal I had been through lift from my shoulders, and it was in a spirit of forgiveness that I asked how I should go about suing the police for wrongful arrest. Dryly, Sergeant informed me that, as technically I had never been cautioned, I therefore had never been under arrest.

'What about when he tried to hit me on the head with his baton?'

Sergeant shook his head non-committally. 'You're out-witnessed. Two of us to one of you, and as it was dark I didn't see what actually happened. And as we experienced on the way here, you can't really call on a lot of character witnesses. So shut up and let me see what it says in this note that was pinned to the roofing up there.' He nodded upwards.

Turning away from me so I could not read the note, he scanned it for a moment before turning round and, with a worried look, handed it to me saying, 'What do you make of that?'

There was a sombre, deadly seriousness in his tone – an indication that I was still in some sort of dire emergency, which rekindled Specky's interest in my welfare.

Crossing over to me he said eagerly, 'Thomething'th up, ithn't there?' His eyes were sparkling again and his voice contained an element of joy that turned to pain when I accidentally stood on his toe and hit his sore arm with my elbow. As he hopped around, trying to hold his toe and arm simultaneously, I read what was written on the note:

TO THE POLICE

Dear Boss
Wot a Jolly time I have had tipping you off.
That joke has given me real fits.
I am down on Ministers and I will give them
a Jolly bad time before I'm throo. HA. HA.
The noking shop was a right wheeze.
I laffd loud when Jolly's woman came down on him
Like a ton of bricks

And all becos of my tipping her off.
My pen is nice and sharp and old misery guts
Can expect more trouble from my tips. Soon.

Yours Truly
Jack the Tipper

I gasped as the letter fell from my grasp and floated gently on a draught to land at the feet of Detective Inspector Sergeant. He bent down and picked it up. My mind was racing in confusion as my life seemed to be taking twists and turns that were bewildering me, and even with my huge capacity to see a cloud behind every silver lining, I admit I was starting to waver.

'What the devil's going on?'

'The Devil might be the very word to use.' Sergeant sat down on a pew and started to fiddle with a hymn-book that had been left from the last service. Nervously, I scrutinised his face for some clue to what was going on behind his thoughtful gaze.

'What do you mean, Detective Inspector, the Devil? I don't understand.'

'Will you shut up,' he shouted.

'I'm entitled to ask,' I replied indignantly.

He paused and from beneath a furrowed brow he snapped, 'Not you – *you*.' He was addressing Poalis, who was still hopping about and clutching his sore arm.

'Thorry, thir,' Poalis sniffed indignantly.

'To answer your question, Reverend, I was on a course once at the Black Museum in Scotland Yard in London.'

'Why do they call it "Scotland Yard" if it's in England?' I asked.

After a brief pause he continued. 'Part of the course involved delving into the records of unsolved cases and it was during this research that I was introduced to the files on the notorious Whitechapel killer, Jack the Ripper.'

'White chapel? So he was a Catholic, then?' I volunteered.

'Shut up!' barked Sergeant.

'I didn't thay a word,' said Poalis.

'Not you – *you*.' Sergeant glared in my direction. I made a motion of zipping up my mouth, which seemed to meet with his approval.

'These files contained amongst other things a letter that was purported to have been written by the Ripper himself, and contained the only clues that the Met had as to his identity.'

'Tho why did the weather people have the clueth and not the poleeth, thir,' said Poalis.

'Weather people?'

'You thaid the Met Offith had the clues to hith identity.'

'*The Metropolitan Police Office* had the clues, not the weather office, you pratt.' I made a motion of zipping up his mouth to Poalis, which he acknowledged – albeit huffily.

Sergeant scratched his head with an air of perplexity. 'What the hell was I saying? You've made me forget, you bloody idiot.'

I stood up to attract his attention. 'You were saying that you were on a course at the Black Museum in London and you were studying the case history of Jack the Ripper, and you came across a letter that was supposed to be written by the Ripper himself, sir.'

'Very good, Jolly, ten out of ten for concentration. You can put your hand down now.'

'Please, sir, what happened next?' I continued, much to the annoyance of Poalis.

'Well. It was written in such a way as to suggest that the writer was from the scruffy side of society. The spelling was wrong and the grammar was so bad that it was said by some observers it was deliberately done to direct the course of the inquiry off the track and lead it off on to another avenue all together.'

'Tho it wath the traffic poleeth who were leading the enquiry, thir?' said Poalis, trying to ingratiate himself and failing miserably.

Sergeant rounded on him and in a voice that suggested he had lost all patience roared, 'Go and stand in the corner. Face the wall and don't come back until you're told.'

Poalis sloped off into the corner and stood there snuffling, snivelling and sobbing to himself.

'The point I'm trying to get at, Jolly, is this. When I was reading the letter a shiver went right up my backbone as I contemplated that I could have been holding the very note that was once composed by the twisted mind of the Ripper. I thought to myself then that I would never again set my eyes on such a letter. And I never have – until now.' He waved the letter under my nose, and with a look that signalled genuine pity, he sighed. 'This letter is so alike in style and content that it could have been written by – Jack the Ripper himself.'

'You mean, you think he might still be alive?' It seemed to me he had lost the plot. 'Surely not, he'd be about two hundred years old,' I laughed.

'Do you want me to send you over beside him?' he scolded. The laughter dried up and I nodded in the negative.

'What I'm trying to tell you is that somewhere out there is someone who dislikes you so much, they are sending anonymous tip-offs to make your life a misery. The signature is Jack the Tipper. That psychotic fixation could develop and lead them on to the conclusion that they are, in fact, Jack the Ripper, and you are to be his or her fated victim.'

As the horror of what Sergeant was saying sunk in, I heard an unearthly chuckle ring round the church.

'It's nothing to laugh about, Poalis,' scolded Sergeant.

As Poalis turned round from facing the wall, he snapped, 'I

126

never laughed.' By the scowl on Poalis's face, it was obvious he was telling the truth.

Sergeant leapt up from the pew and raced down the aisle and out the front door.

'Eh, the toilet is inside, to your left just past the porch,' I called after him.

Turning to Poalis, I explained that it might be the cold weather and the dampness of the church and how it sometimes had the same effect on me. I had started to let him in on the secret precaution I take if I am, shall we say, caught short during a sermon. It's my practice to always keep two bottles of limeade – one empty and one with some limeade in it – secreted behind the pulpit. This way, I can always have a drink when I'm thirsty. However, the down side of this is that inevitably I want to do the toilet – which is where the other bottle comes in handy, if you get my meaning.

I was explaining to him that limeade was best because the colouring was particularly suitable if it was discovered by accident, when Detective Inspector Sergeant burst in through the front door and informed us, rather breathlessly as he ran down the aisle, 'No sign of them. Is there a back door out of here?'

'Well, yes!' I replied, quite mystified as to what was going on. 'There's one over there. You won't see it from here, it's hidden behind the pulpit.'

I could tell he was irritated by the way he shoved me on my sit-upon as he barged past on his way round the pulpit to the back door.

'Is this door usually locked?' he shouted as the door sprung open at his touch.

'Yes, there's no need for it to be opened during the week,' I called out as he closed the door behind him and walked back towards me, stroking his chin thoughtfully.

'Damn, that's how they got away then. Did you see

anything, Poalis?'

'*No!* If you remember, I wath told to thtand in the corner and fathe the wall. Tho how could I thee if I wath told not to look, thir.' He really was petulance personified now as he turned back round to face the wall and started to kick the toes of his shoes against it.

Sergeant moved over towards him and stood beside him for a while before laying a sympathetic hand on his shoulder. Patting him on the back, he murmured softly, 'Point taken. Alright?'

Poalis nodded affirmatively without looking round.

'Good lad,' said Sergeant, giving Poalis's arm an affectionate squeeze. 'Now stop kicking the wall – you'll scuff your shoes – and come over and join us.'

As he led Poalis towards me, I tried to make some sense of what was going on. Even Ephesia's company was beginning to look quite inviting compared with what I had been through recently.

I sat down and said a wee prayer. 'God. If you can spare a minute, I could use some help. It's not convenient to talk at the moment as I'm with someone. But I'll get back to you later. Cheerybye.'

Sergeant sat down and seemed to stare into space before pronouncing, 'Judging by the fact that you didn't laugh, I didn't laugh and neither did constable Poalis, it would not be too much of a leap of logic to surmise that whoever did laugh also wrote this note. This means we have a full-blown stalker on our hands.' He paused as if gathering his thoughts. 'I ran out to see if I could catch a glimpse of – whoever it was – but no luck. The stalker must have been hiding inside the pulpit when we first arrived. They waited inside the pulpit to make sure we discovered the letter, obviously to find out if his or her actions had the desired effect. If only I had ran the right way when I heard that strange laugh we might have caught him. Damn.'

'Hold on a minute,' said Poalis. His face seemed to be contorted in pain, so I presumed he was trying to think.

'Is something the matter, Poalis?' Sergeant asked earnestly.

'I'm jutht trying to think, thir. Reverend Jolly? You told me that you thometimeth keep an empty bottle in the pulpit in cathe you need a pith. Ith that right?'

I could not help but notice the look of surprise that Sergeant's face registered as he eased himself away from me. Nevertheless, I was duty bound to answer the question.

'Well, two actually. Most preachers have some form of receptacle to help them through those, emm! – shall we say – difficult moments? If you suddenly have to go, you can't just leave people hanging in the middle of a sermon. The Jews have the Pass Over, so I have the Piss Into. Mind you, the noise can be a bit of a give-away, so I usually suggest a sing-along. "Bridge Over Troubled Waters" usually does the trick. The louder the better. But I don't see what that has to do with me being stalked.'

Sergeant turned to look at Poalis and said with what I thought was an unnecessary firmness in his tone, 'This better be good, Poalis.'

'Work with me on thith, thir. It might be of thignificanth. If the mithcreant wath hiding in the pulpit, like you thay, then maybe – jutht maybe – he touched the bottle and . . .'

'*Of course!*' Sergeant interrupted. 'He may have left fingerprints. Brilliant, Poalis, just brilliant. Jolly, did you leave a bottle there?'

I answered right away. 'Yes. Parson's throat can be quite nasty. I remember one time . . .'

'Yes, yes,' he interrupted. 'Never mind that, let's have a look.'

We dashed towards the pulpit and practically flew round to the short set of stairs that leads up to the pulpit floor. Sure enough, there was my customary bottle on the floor propped up against the inside of the pulpit.

'We're in luck, thir,' Poalis exclaimed.

Sergeant punched the air with his fist. 'Yes!' he yelled. 'Poalis – get this down to the lab and we'll go over it for fingerprints. The note's useless, paper too cheap, won't hold a print.'

'You really think the bottle could help, Detective Inspector?' I asked, as Poalis ascended the pulpit. Sergeant's eyes were fixed on Poalis as he bent down to pick up the bottle.

'Wear a glove!' he instructed. 'Yes, Reverend, it might just be the clue that wraps the whole thing up.'

Poalis informed us that he did not have his gloves with him, however he said he would put on one of mine that he'd found in the pulpit – a woolly one. Using the glove, he started to lift the bottle. As he was doing so I remembered that I didn't have a woolly glove. Poalis remarked as he was holding the bottle that the glove was soaking wet due to my not having dried the outside of the bottle where I had spilled the lime after taking a drink. I thought I should mention the glove thing, in case it was important.

'Can I just say I never wear gloves. Oh, and can I also say I never drink from that bottle because it's not lime that's in that bottle. That's the piss into bottle. Sorry, I should maybe have explained the difference. That may not be lime, it may be . . .'

'*Aaagghh!*' Poalis dropped the bottle and ran up to the baptismal font, where he thrust his now glove-less hand into the water.

'There'th lime in here too,' he howled, washing his hand.

'No, that should be water,' I said.

'Well, itth green . . . *Aaagghh!*' he screamed again, running out the church and shoving his hand into a large puddle that was lying on the ground. I told Sergeant that I couldn't understand why the piss into bottle had any p— ehh, liquid in it as I always emptied it.

As we surveyed the by-now smashed bottle, Sergeant was deep in thought. Turning to me, he explained that it was my stalker who had supplied the liquid in the bottle – also the liquid in the font – and that he had deliberately left the wet glove so that whoever tried it on would realise their mistake, drop the bottle in disgust, and thus destroy the evidence.

Crossing to the font, he placed his finger in the liquid and lifted it to his nose. I watched in fascination as he sniffed at it, then I almost gagged as he tasted it.

'Yes,' he smiled wryly. 'As I thought. He's gone for the double bluff. It's lime. We are dealing with a very clever criminal here.'

I T WAS LATE AFTERNOON when I arrived back at the manse. I decided a nice hot cup of tea would help to calm me down a bit and I put the kettle on to boil. While I was waiting for that to happen I went over what Sergeant had advised me. He suggested that I supply him with a list of people who I thought might bear me enough ill will to make them act the way the anonymous tipper-come-stalker had. I said I would try to think of someone who fitted that description, but it would be difficult because, as a minister, it was my job to befriend the laity not antagonise them. He surprised me by insisting that I might be amazed by the outcome of such an exercise.

The kettle whistled its cheerful warning that it had boiled and the water was now ready to be transformed into tea by simply adding a tea-bag. Opening the tea-caddy I saw that there was a scarcity of tea bags – in fact, they were so scarce there were none. There was, however, a note inside.

I thought to myself, 'That's a bit odd, I've never seen a note in the tea-caddy before.' Then it hit me.

'The Tipper. He's been in the manse.' My voice echoed round the kitchen, and I staggered a bit before finally composing myself. Sergeant had told me to inform him of any new development as soon as it happened so my first thought was to phone him.

As I waited for him to answer the phone, I stared nervously at the note, which was still in the tea-caddy. The receiver was finally picked up at the police station.

'Yeth. Thith ith the poleeth. Who ith thith calling uth?'

'Is that you, Constable Poalis?' I asked, unnecessarily. 'This is the Reverend I. M. Jolly here.'

I heard him say gloomily, 'Oh jobbies,' so I corrected him. 'No, it's "Jolly". My name is not "Jobbies".'

He said, 'It ith in here.'

After advising him to amend his records, I asked to be put

through to Sergeant.

The day's work seemed to have taken its toll on Sergeant's health and vitality as I could hear him say in the background, 'Tell him I'm sick and tired of him! Oh, never mind, pass the phone over. Yes, Reverend Jolly, what can I do for you?'

'The Tipper has been in my house and left a note,' I said quickly.

I heard him whistle softly through his teeth. 'That's a new and – if I may say so – very disturbing turn of events. What does it say?'

'I haven't read it yet,' I told him. 'You said to phone you right away if anything occurred.'

'So I did, that's right,' he mumbled to himself. 'Where is it now?'

'It's in the tea-caddy,' I explained.

After a pause he asked, with a slight hint of incredulity in his voice, 'Why did you put it in the tea-caddy?'

I explained that I didn't put it in the tea-caddy, that I had found it there.

'Go to the tea-caddy, lift the note out – use a piece of tissue paper so you don't spoil any fingerprints that may be on it – and read what it says. I'll send a squad car round immediately. In case you are – not alone? I should lock all the doors in the house till we get there. After you've done that, read me what the swine has written.'

Quickly, I locked the front door and, after checking that the back door was also secure, tore off a piece of kitchen roll to handle the letter with. It was folded in two. I did not dare unfold it to read what was writ on it in case I passed out, so I picked up the phone and said to Sergeant that I had it in my hand.

My breathing had become more laboured, however he tried to calm me by talking me through the ordeal I was about to undergo. His voice was indeed an oasis in the desert that had become my kitchen. I could feel myself relax.

'Have you locked all the doors?'

I grunted assent.

'And have you also checked that there is no one hiding behind the curtains, or inside the wall cupboards, or even under the table maybe?'

I could feel myself tense up again. Isn't it funny how, when your whole body tenses, the only thing that slackens are your bowels.

'Do you think I could go and do the bathroom, Detective Inspector?' I said in a pleading sort of way.

'Have you checked it out?' he said quietly.

'I'm afraid not,' I answered.

'In that case, you'll just have to clench your teeth and get on with reading the note.'

I decided that my teeth were not in as an immediate need of clenching as one other part of my body, however I also decided that this was not a decision that I needed to share with anyone but me.

Steeling my resolve not to panic and not to evacuate, I fished out the note from inside the tea cosy with the aid of the kitchen roll fragment and transported it to the waiting telephone. Putting the note down I picked up the telephone.

'I have the note here,' I said into the phone while at the same time nervously looking round the room to make sure that The Tipper was not going to jump out at me from under the table or out of a cupboard.

'Read it, Jolly.' There was a commanding note in the timbre of Sergeant's voice that made me obey even though I passionately did not want to.

'I'm unfolding it now,' I said.

'Careful not to spoil any fingerprints,' he reminded me.

'It's unfolded,' I said, still not daring to read it.

'Good, Jolly. You're doing fine. Now *read it.*'

With my voice and my hands trembling, I began to read.

We have run out of tea.
I've gone to the shops
Use the coffee that we keep for visitors till I get back

Ephesia

PS
We've no milk either so you needn't bother looking for it.
PPS
I think my course in calligraphy is beginning to pay off.

As the sound of my front door being broken down by a police battering-ram manifested itself in my ears, I could faintly make out what I took to be Poalis's voice in the background saying, 'Lettis Bootim Upis Rectum.' I don't speak Latin, so I must ask my good friend Father Knox what it means.

A FTER THE EVENTS OF YESTERDAY I need some activity to take me out of myself and, more importantly, restore me to my normal jovial lifestyle. Fortunately, I have always found that preparing my sermon for Sunday services has never failed to perk me up. At all costs I must not let my flock see that I am down in spirits, so I'll just nip round to the off-licence for a wee half-bottle.

Having fortified myself for the task ahead with a large dram, I must set out the tone of my text. I'll start by showing an example to them on how not to let things get on top of you. Here goes.

Hullo! It's lovely to see you all. I must say the pair of you are looking marvellous.

Now, you're probably saying, 'What's he got to be so cheerful about?' Well, don't be taken in by this apparent air of skittishness that I give out – like many of you there are times when I sit down and suffer pain and anxiety. However, I bring good news. You can get an ointment that will clear it up.

Although I am smiling away here, I must tell you I have had one hell of a week. It has been full of sadness, despondency, gloom and rejection. But all this misery and suffering can be used and turned into something worthwhile and positive. It has allowed me to put myself in the shoes of others. At least, I now know what it must be like to be in *EastEnders*.

Also there were good and bad points to the week. Inevitably there were some things I'm glad I done and some things I wish I'd never done.

And speaking of Ephesia, she has been there for me no matter what. A rock. In fact, she reminds me of the apostle Peter – six feet two, with a heavy growth and smelling of fish.

I can still remember the words of my old theology teacher Deuteronomy MacBride: 'Why waste time and energy getting yourself depressed. Get out there amongst the people and get them depressed.' As I think I've mentioned before, he was a bit off the wall. He was also off his head but that's another story.

(Around about now I usually have a swig of limeade, but I'm going to cut that as I'm a bit wary.)

Ephesia, as I say, has been like a ray of sunshine, but even she can get down in the dumps – and, of course, it's up to me to spot the little tell-tale signs that mean she is not happy. For example, last Monday when I came home, there were my slippers waiting for me – in the fridge.

Sometimes if you're very low a holiday can help. I well remember going on a cut-price flight to – well, I'm not quite sure where we went. That was why it was cut price *of course*, because that's where we went – *off course*.

I do admit to a degree of dubiety as to the wisdom of booking the flight when I saw the plane. It wasn't just the fact that it only had the one wing, it was more the German Cross that was painted on the wing that made me wonder. That – coupled with the fact that we had to push it downhill to start it – worried me.

What a fright the flight furnished up. The thing went up, down, sideways, upside down, every which way but forward. The captain said he was having trouble with the turbulence and the wind. I am here to tell you he was not the only one. People began to panic and shout we're all going to die – and that was the crew.

The captain shouted to me, 'You're a minister, do something.' So I took up a collection.

There were two children running up and down the aisle getting in everyone's way. I could sense they might be in danger from hysterical passengers, so I opened the door and told them to play outside for a while. The mother called me for everything. However, that stopped when she went out to look for them.

Eventually the wind that was holding us up in the air stopped and we managed to land the plane. I remember thinking as we disembarked that at last the fun was starting: it was the first time I'd slid down a chute since I was a boy.

The hotel was bright and airy, due to the fact it was only half-built and had no roof. And although it boasted there were two hundred beds, it neglected to say they were all in the same room.

Ephesia got into the holiday mood straightaway and said she was going to go topless. I got very excited. I thought she was going to cut her head off. There was also a beautiful seventeen-and-a-half-hole golf course that they'd built just a bit too near the sea and I suggested to Ephesia that we play a round. Fortunately, she said she had a headache.

But I remember one day I sat gazing out to the ocean, wondering if I could build a raft, and it set me to thinking of Noah and his family and the problems they encountered. Noah was just an ordinary man with an extraordinary number of pets, which was to come in handy later on in his life. He had three sons – Sham, Hem and Japheth. Now, it came to pass that Hem had a face like a bag of chisels, and when people saw Sham and Hem about together they would say, 'That's a sham about hem, isn't it.' And Noah's other son, Japheth, had a fondness for biscuits and cakes and oft did make a pig of himself. His favourite sweet things were cakes made from a small round biscuit with orange jelly on top and the jelly was then covered in chocolate. Indeed, he was so fond of them that they were known throughout the land as Japheth's cakes.

One day his sons ran to Noah and said, 'There's a flood,' and Noah said unto them, 'Well, who let the dog in the living-room?' 'No, father,' they said, 'it's going to rain for forty days and forty nights,' and Noah's wife said, 'I'd better get the washing in then.'

And Noah was told to build a vessel three hundred cubits long, fifty cubits wide and thirty cubits high. And Noah was vexed because he normally worked in feet and inches. And Noah's calculations were well out and lo, he did make an ark of it, and Noah was six hundred years old when the floodwaters rose. (He was actually forty-two but building the ark took a lot out of him.)

So it came to pass that Noah and his family and all his pets went on the first Cunard cruise round the world and they deserved it because they'd all worked for-Cunard.

And Noah sent forth a dove, and the dove returned with an olive. And Noah knew that the earth had dried up and there was a delicatessen opened somewhere. And the Lord said unto Noah and his family, 'No more will I flood the earth. For you are a good and righteous man. And as a reward I will send a bow in the sky and it shall have all the colours of the rainbow in it. In fact, that's no' a bad name. I will call it a 'rainbow' and it will be my covenant with you.'

And so God Almighty made the rainbow and it was a thing of joy and beauty. Then someone called a television producer – who thought he was God Almighty – added Jeffrey, Zippy and Bungle to the rainbow and made a fortune.

I SAT DOWN THIS MORNING and at the behest of Detective Inspector Sergeant tried to think of someone – *anyone* – who disliked me. Try as I might I just could not think of a single person who fitted the bill. I even sat in my favourite armchair. I always use it if I have to think through a problem and it never fails to help me come up with a solution. Father had given it to me as a wedding present when Ephesia and I tied the knot. His father had bequeathed it to him and it held so many fond memories for me: sitting astride one of the arms and pretending to be a cowboy on a horse, chasing Red Indians across the plains, firing an imaginary rifle, pretending to be injured by an imaginary arrow, and falling off the arm of the chair fatally wounded. Lying on the carpet dead. Then, as only the mind of a four-year-old can conjure up, a miraculous recovery would take place and, leaping back on the arm of the chair, father would again be on the trail of 'those pesky Redskins', as he used to call them.

Sometimes he would even let me be an Indian and he would hunt me down, tie me to a tree in the garden and then scalp me before setting fire to the dead branches he had placed under my feet. It was only when I grew up I realised it should have been the other way round, but father was never one to let historical accuracy stand in the way of him having fun with his son. Such was his enthusiasm that one time he even dug a hole and placed my mother in it so only her head was above the ground. Then, laying a trail of jam from an ants' nest to under Mum's chin, he waited to see if they would eat her alive, as he'd seen them do to a bit-part player in a John Wayne film. He realised he'd gone too far, of course, when mother pointed out to him that it was nearly dinner-time and she still hadn't put the potatoes on to boil.

Shaking his head, he looked at Ranald and I and muttered, 'Women?' We all knew he was very angry but not being the sort of man to bear a grudge he dug her out. He was too much of a realist to ignore the fact that he would have to have made the dinner himself, and of course, that was woman's work.

As I look back with fond memories of my childhood, I now see that what we were doing under father's guidance was bonding as a family. Sometimes I wonder if in our haste to be modernist and politically correct, we haven't lost something of those old-fashioned values. They are, after all, what made me what I am today.

It was during my reveries on this theme that Ranald paid me one of his impromptu visits. I could hear the wood on the front doorframe crack under the pressure of a size twelve hobnail and I knew instinctively that he was in one of his moods.

The living-room door flew open. Standing there, with his boots encased in the mud from a freshly dug grave and a wreath hanging round his neck, he stared at me inquisitively.

'Are you wanting to come out to play, or not?'

'I'm afraid that I can't right now, Ranald. I have quite a lot on my mind.' I tried not to be too evasive in my response as I didn't want to spoil his day by burdening my troubles on to him.

'Can I help?' he offered, as he absentmindedly started to unravel a coffin tassel that he'd fished out from one of the pockets of his long, black frock-coat. I knew instinctively that this was a silent cry for help I was witnessing. When Ranald was grieving in his spirit, he always wore the undertaker's outfit that he'd got for his twelfth birthday. It had always been one of father's tenets that everyone should have a hobby, and Ranald's was coffin-spotting. In fact, he used to get very annoyed that undertakers did not put numbers on coffins. His argument was that train-spotters had therefore an unfair advantage over coffin-spotters. He tried to form a pressure group of him, father and me to lobby undertakers not only to number their various coffins, but also to give them names after the fashion of trains. He suggested that, if a train could be called *The Flying Scotsman*, then a coffin could be, for example, *The Totally Still Scotsman*. Father – always one to encourage us – tried to set up Corpses R Us as a feeder for Ranald's hobby, but it never got off the ground, never mind under it.

Ranald looked up from his task of unravelling the coffin tassel and, glancing over my shoulder at the full-length mirror on the wall, he studied himself intently. Starting from his feet, his gaze trawled up his body until his eyes came to rest on his head. With a sigh of deep melancholy, he turned his face away from me so I would not see the disappointment that was registered there. This was a regular occurrence with my dear brother when he looked at a mirror because, although he never said as much to me, I knew that in his heart of hearts he lived in hope that one day he would have no reflection – which would mean he'd be dead. Unfortunately, today was not that day. I felt heart sorry for him because, if it had been, that would definitely have given him a lift.

I reasoned that if I shared my own particular problem with him, then maybe it would cheer him up and make him think that life was not so bad after all. Not, of course, in Ranald's eyes as good as death, but you can only play with the cards you are holding.

'Ranald?' I said questioningly, 'I know this might sound a silly question, to which you will probably not be able to supply an answer, but can you? Now don't laugh,' I said, finding that I was smiling myself because the question was so preposterous. 'Can you think of anyone who dislikes me?'

'Hundreds,' he said, staring wistfully at the mirror again.

Now, I have to admit that even I never supposed that Ranald had such a waggish sense of humour, but it was good to know that my talent for getting folk to see the funny side of life was still actively engaging my fellow man.

'No, seriously,' I said, 'I have been asked to write down a list of people who might –' again a smile played round the corners of my mouth, '– who might dislike me. So no larking about now, can you think of anyone – however unlikely – who might find me even a teeny-weenie bit objectionable?'

'Hundreds,' he replied again, with a straight face as he waved at his reflection.

'Now look, Ranald,' I said. 'This is serious, OK? Between you and me and the lamppost, is there anyone – and I know you're starting to lose the air of melancholy you had when you came in, and I like a joke and appreciate your pawky sense of humour as much as the next one – but I would ask you to concentrate and try, hard as it may be, try to think of . . .'

'Hundreds,' he interrupted me as he got down on the floor and, placing two coins on his eyes, he lay prone with his hands folded on his chest. 'I'm going to stop breathing for a while,' he intoned. 'If I achieve a state of coma, don't spoil it for me, OK?'

He took a deep breath, then let it out, and with a marvellously real impression of a death rattle (which he had perfected in his younger days and was now justifiably proud of), he lay anaesthetised to the world. This was Ranald's way of not coping with things that he couldn't cope with. His reasoning was that whereas most of us were terrified of dying, he had made dying his life's ambition, and unlike most of us who have ambitions that never came to much, he was sure of fulfilling his.

There was no point in interrupting him as he could only hold his breath for about a minute and a bit, after which he would start to redden up and be forced to take a breath. Then he would get up off the floor, cross to the mirror and check if he was still visible. I knew he would need cheering up after finding out he was still alive, so I decided to make a cup of tea for us both.

When I returned to the living-room with tea and Abernethy biscuits, Ranald had gone through his routine and seemed to be over the worst of his disappointment.

'No luck?' I said sympathetically.

Ranald looked up and as he shook his head replied, 'Just have to grin and bear it, I suppose.' He perked up immediately he saw the Abernethy biscuits. Grabbing a cup of tea, he sat on the top of the sideboard. 'What was it you were asking me about?' he said, polishing the top of the sideboard with his biscuit. He realised what he was doing and sheepishly said, 'What am I like, trying to polish the sideboard with an Abernethy biscuit?'

I was glad reason was taking over again. He waved it in the air. 'I mean, honestly, an Abernethy biscuit that hasn't been dipped into the tea. How's that supposed to clean a sideboard? There are times I wonder about myself, I really do.'

As he set about cleaning the sideboard with a sodden Abernethy biscuit, I decided to have one more go as to whether he could think of anyone who would wish me ill.

'Hundreds,' he repeated.

I thought to myself, right, dear brother, I'm going to put you on the spot here.

'Hundreds, you say, eh? Alright, I'm going to ask you to name some, OK? Take your time. I'll give you an hour to collect your thoughts then I want you to come up with some names. Fair enough?'

'Me.'

'Yes you! Who else is there in the room?

'No. I mean me. *I* don't like you. Then there's father, he thinks you're a pain in the arse. Ephesia worship's the ground you'll be buried under. Old Mr Crabbit would gladly see you snuff it. R. Sinparsley says you stole newspapers from him and would like you locked up in Gaddafi's Café to keep Al Whatsisname company. Then there's the entire staff of that restaurant you go to and don't tip anyone. The postman. And I heard you nearly drowned a baby at some christening, so there's a mother and father that we can add to the list.'

I must say I was verging on total trauma as he assailed my

ears with this barrage of adversaries. Surely he was exaggerating. Ranald could have a keen and biting side to his wit and was not averse to sending me up from time to time.

Of course, that was it: he was indulging in typical Ranald banter, and I – in my present state of vulnerability – had fallen for his joshing. *Ah me!* He really caught me on the ropes this time.

'Then I heard you were singing at a funeral and upset the mourners. There's a rumour the Synod of the Church of Scotland want rid of you. Oh, and Virago and Madonna are thinking of suing you over sexist remarks you made at another christening. And then there's . . .'

'OK. I've twigged what you're up to.' I wagged my finger knowingly in his face. 'You got me going there.'

'Mother used to have a soft spot for you, but then eventually you got on her nerves as well,' Ranald continued as I led him out the door. 'Are there not two old biddies that still turn up on a Sunday? At a stretch they might find you bearable, then again . . .'

I shut the door on him, still silently chuckling to myself at how easily Ranald had punctured my vanity and how in his innocence he had also shown me the folly of taking myself too seriously.

Feeling much better, I noticed Ranald hadn't quite finished his tea, so never being one to indulge in waste I picked it up, had a wee gulp and then flopped down on my old armchair and settled down for a read at the newspaper.

'BRITISH HOSPITALS IN CHAOS', was the headline. Well, I thought, I'm not in the mood to be depressed, so on to the next page. 'BRITISH RAILWAYS A SHAMBLES'. Oh dear! Next page then. 'SCOTTISH WATER DIRTIEST IN EUROPE'. That one put me off my tea. Try again. 'SCOTTISH ROADS A DISGRACE'. There must be some good news. 'MSPs AWARD THEMSELVES HUGE PAY-RISE TO KEEP UP WITH BRITISH

MPs'.

Dear God Almighty, I thought to myself (but not in a blasphemous way), if Jesus was alive today He'd be giving them what for, the way He had done in the temple with the moneylenders. Mind you, at least the temple moneylenders loaned you *their* money. This lot just whip your own money off you and then toss it around like confetti at a wedding – which is bad enough – but on top of that it's always *their* weddings that they're tossing our money at. It's only my opinion but the facts seem to prove they're a right bunch of tossers.

As I was fuming away, another article caught my eye: 'KIRK'S HYMNS HIT BY POLITICAL CORRECTNESS'. The article went on to say that the Church of Scotland was going to ditch many of its traditional hymns because they were out of date and were deemed not politically correct enough for the modern age.

My first thought was one of indignation at the prospect of casting aside the hymns I had been brought up with. Then an idea began to form in my brain. Why not compose a hymn that reflected what was going on round about our very lives? A hymn that was relevant to today's problems. A hymn that spoke for the common man and how modern living was affecting him (and her, of course. My God, I'm into this modern way of thinking already). This would show that I was in tandem with the Church's thinking, that I was modern in my approach to the religion of today, that I was a caring pastor and that I should not be given the ecclesiastical bullet but the minister's medal of modern monotheism and an increase in salary. I could almost feel my stipend rise at the thought of it.

Leaping out of the chair I crossed the room to my desk, threw open the drawer and rummaged around till I found a pencil with a rubber on the end of it. That's the first part of my plan completed, I gloated, as I fished out the pencil. Phase two? A bit of writing-paper! My trusty notepad sprang to mind. Gotcha! Phase three, write a modern hymn that will revolutionise the entire way of Church thinking and set the tone for the new millennium. Hmmm – this might require some thought before I actually commit pencil to paper.

What should the tune be like unto? Why not 'The Lord's My Shepherd'? Why Not! I began to write, singing the tune to myself.

> As I walked to the church one day
> On a paving slab I did trip
> I've been waiting now – nearly two years –
> For an operation on my hip.
>
> I'm waiting here on platform two
> I'm going on my holiday
> Well maybe not – it's just been announced
> The trains are on strike today.
>
> I thirsted for knowledge – and for love
> My heart knew not which way to choose
> I took a drink – of Scottish tap water –
> And was sick – all over my shoes.
>
> In the chariot of life – I did ride
> I needed to save my soul
> But I was thrown out – of the chariot of life
> When the wheel hit a big pothole.
>
> I had no money – I had no food
> I had no clothes – and no footwear
> I met an angel – who stole them from me
> He said, trust me – I'm Tony Blair.
>
> AH! –MEN

I hummed over the words to myself a few times to make sure they fitted exactly with the melody, and I must say they did, like unto a glove, in fact. Then I started to wonder if I should not only update the meaning of the Church's message by altering the words, but also by altering the melody as well. Why the Devil should the Devil have all the best tunes to himself?

As I began to develop the idea further, I started to see the possibilities open up. What if I sparked a worldwide revival of the Church of Scotland? I felt another inspirational moment spark into life inside my brain. I could imagine myself at the Synod, waiting in the wings as Wilson Simmons himself spoke to a packed throng of cheering churchmen.

'Fellow reverends, we have all had a marvellous annual get-together.'

Wild cheering.

'This has been without doubt the most successful year ever in the history of the Church of Scotland. Attendances are so high we are having to build more kirks throughout the land.'

The noise from the throng starts to swell. Wilson tries in vain to quieten the exhilarated crowd but he has to shout to make himself heard.

'Our leader, the Moderator of the Church of Scotland, is delighted to be here today to welcome the man who has made this dream come true. Using nothing but the sheer raw talent given to him by God, he has single-handedly changed the course of our Church from potential extinction to *the* most potent force for good in the world today.'

Hats are thrown into the air; the massed throng around the stadium begins to chant, *'We want Jolly! We want Jolly!'*

With his arms splayed towards the heavens, Wilson Simmons, now unfettered by the old Church of Scotland restrictions, cries out in ecstasy. 'You want him?'

The mob scream back, *'Yes!'*

Wilson's voice has now ascended to the firmament. 'You've

got him. Reverends and Reverendesses, *here he is! The Reverend I. M. JOLLY!'*

As the stadium erupts, I hang back a little, letting the tension build. Then, just when everyone is starting to wonder why I haven't appeared . . . I walk modestly towards the centre of the stage, one hand raised to the assembly in a gesture of salutation and solidarity. Then, as I reach the centre and the solo spotlight settles on my face, I nod my head in a tiny gesture of acknowledgement that sends the audience into raptures, and – throwing both arms aloft – I shout to them, 'I HAVE A NEW HYMN. WOULD YOU LIKE TO HEAR IT?'

I smile shyly when they go mad with delight as Bibles are thrown on to the stage, and ambulance crews have to move in to remove some female ministers for whom the excitement has proved too much.

'THIS IS MY TRIBUTE TO THE MODERATOR OF THE CHURCH OF SCOTLAND.' I wave to the Moderator and he acknowledges my gesture by raising his arms and clasping his hands together above his head in a triumphant but not showing-off-at-all sort of way that still has the crowd in a frenzy. 'THIS ONE'S ON ME, MODDY!' I shout out, punching the air.

The Salvation orchestra strikes up and to the tune of 'Hello Dolly' I go into the performance.

> *Hello, Moderator, I said hello, Moderator*
> *It's so nice that we are back where we belong*
> *It's really so thrilling, to see the kirks filling*
> *We're still praying, we're still saying*
> *We're the Church of Scotland throng.*
>
> *Other churches' flocks are slumping*
> *But our pews they are jumping*
> *With the happy slappy sound of a bum on a seat*

So on your knees, sinners
We're the bees knees and we're the winners
Cause Moderator we're back on our feet.

The orchestra slows in tempo and vamps its way into the big finish with the brass section sending out its rhythmic message of, *'Pam a pam amapam amapam pam'*. And I'm right in there, my voice sailing along on top of the wave Sinatra-style as I end with:

We're not empty, we're replete . . . papapam
Now our songs of praise are all upbeat . . . papapam
Cause Moderator we are on our feet agaiiin.

Then a huge back cloth is lowered on to the stage with the words written on it. The massed voices of the Church of Scotland Synod choir fills the auditorium and balloons in the shape of little kirks are dropped from the roof of the auditorium. As I stroll off I stop, turn, and with a cheery wave wish them all, 'Good night and God bless.' Mass hysteria follows.

'Yes. That way lies the future,' I said aloud, such was my enthusiasm for the venture.

As I searched for an envelope, I could imagine the Synod's reaction when they received my offering. I surmised that the phrase 'Hymns Ancient and Modern' would no longer be applicable. It would have to be modern and even more modern now. They may even want me to cut a record. (I believe that is the jargon in Tin Pan Alley these days.)

I was toying with the idea of arranging singing lessons when the front doorbell rang.

Still humming 'Hello Moderator' to myself as I traversed the hallway, I opened the door and saw that, strangely enough, there was no one there. I stepped outside to scrutinise a bit further but, despite my best efforts, there was definitely a distinct absence of humankind. A noticeable chill hung in the air and I perceived that even though it was still relatively early in the afternoon there was a gloominess settling into the day which was at odds to my own high spirits – or, to put it another way, 'It was gey dreich, but the sun shone oot my hin-end.'

Chuckling at my observation, I turned to go back inside having decided that I must have imagined the doorbell. As I did I saw that there was a note pinned to the door. Remembering the embarrassment of the last time when I wrongly thought that Ephesia's note was from my stalker, I decided not to contact the police this time. With great trepidation, I took away the pin from the door and opened the note. It read as follows:

Dear Reverend Jolly

I have heard from a friend that you are being stalked. And that someone has been sending notes containing lies about you. This fiend calls himself Jack the Tipper. Well this note is not from him. It's from your milkman who you never tip. Your wife asked me to leave an extra pint, so here it is on your doorstep.

PS Watch you don't trip over it.

Unfortunately, as I turned to see if there was indeed a bottle of milk, I inadvertently caught it with the edge of my foot. It fell from the step and broke, spilling its contents on to the ground.

'Hell,' I blasphemed, Ephesia would gut me now. The only thing for it was to clear it up quickly before she got back and then deny all knowledge that it had ever been there.

Racing into the kitchen I argued with myself that, although I would be telling a lie, it would be a white one and that God in His infinite mercy would sympathise with me on this one. In a bit of a panic, I lifted up a brush and shovel and headed for the door. Then I realised I would need a cloth or mop to wipe away the spilled milk. I knew there was a cloth in the cupboard under the sink, so rushing back into the kitchen I flung open the cupboard door and grabbed the cloth then hurried back to the front door, praying that Ephesia would not arrive in time to catch me out.

I was in luck – there was no sign of her. Stooping down to clean up the mess, I noticed something odd. Beside the broken bottle of milk there was now a cat; it had traces of milk on its whiskers. It was also now – a dead cat. It was also now time to phone the police – again.

I heard the receiver being picked up and a voice answered: 'Yeth. Thith ith the poleeth. Who ith thith?'

'It's me, the Reverend I. M. Jolly.'

It seemed as if Poalis was instructing someone not to stand, because I'm sure I heard him say, '*Oh thyitt!*'

'Someone's tried to murder me,' I informed him.

His instructions must have been successful for I heard him say, 'Great, it'th about time.'

WHILE I WAS WAITING for the police to arrive, I nipped down to the post-box at the corner of the street and posted my suggestions for the updated hymnal. I really did feel that even if The Tipper got to me, at least the world should not be deprived of my *magnum opus*.

Hurriedly I deposited the letter in the post-box – or, as it used to be called, the Consignia container. No doubt the guardians of our welfare will decide to rename the post office again and some public relations company will cop another couple of million from the bottomless pit that politicians call the 'public purse'. I read somewhere that 'poly' means many and 'tics' are blood-sucking lice. I'm digressing again, but can you blame me?

I think I may have been talking to myself as well. The reason I think I may have been talking to myself is that I caught me giving myself a round of applause after the observation about blood-sucking parasitical parliamentarians. I may be heading for a breakdown.

I feared a panic attack imminent. I feared it because as I approached the manse I could just see Ephesia pull up outside on her tandem. (I used to cycle with her but she went too fast and my ankles were always getting bruised from the flying pedals that assaulted them.)

As she swept through the gate up to the front door, I called out to her, 'Hello, petal. Eh, if you see a dead cat at the front doorstep it's not my fault.'

Ephesia had indeed spotted the deceased, and the milk that was now starting to stain the paving slab. She turned slowly to face me as I slithered through the gate and then stood nervously with my hands in my pockets, looking at the ground and trying to feign a casual approach to the scene of the crime.

She made towards me. I jumped behind a fortuitously placed silver birch tree that was suffering from powdery mildew – which, although rare in a birch, can be treated by repeated spraying with a benlate compound of . . . Bugger! I'm digressing again! I can't seem to control –

Ephesia's voice cut through my thoughts as she took up a position on the other side of the tree. 'Don't tell me Ranald's practising voodoo again! And take your hands out of your pockets. What have I told you about fiddling with yourself when you're nervous? Well, answer me.'

I started to stammer out a reply, then I inadvertently caught her eye and could see she was going to lose patience with me. So, taking a breath to control my thoughts, I said with a firmness of purpose which actually came out as a nervous laugh, 'No, my little pigeon, Ranald's not back on the voodoo again, though it is entirely understandable that you thought so.' My nervous laugh turned to a nervous whine.

'Stop crawling and explain yourself. You know I get really annoyed when you start to crawl and you're whining as well. How many times have I told you? Don't whine!' she snapped, stripping the bark off of the tree with her fingernails. 'I won't ask you again. What happened here?'

'Someone has tried to poison me,' I blurted out. 'He's called Jack the Tipper and he started off by sending poison pen letters tipping people off that I'd been up to no good.' I saw her make a start to lunge at me. 'He was lying, honestly. You received one, my pumpkin. The massage parlour, remember?' I explained in the nick of time.

The muscles on her neck relaxed again and I knew I was safe for the moment, so I hurried on. 'Well, it seems that Jack the Tipper has identified with Jack the Ripper, or so the police told me when they took me to the police station the other day.' I saw her hackles rise again and I knew I had to talk fast. 'Because this madman who is stalking me had left a threatening note which threatened me, so the police wanted to protect me from the poison pen letters, but now he's gone a step further and tried to poison *me*. Luckily, however, the cat got poisoned instead of me. This man's wrath has terrified me, Ephesia, I'm in a terrible state and my nerves are shot to pieces.'

Try as I might I could not stop a solitary tear from rolling down my cheek and into the corner of my mouth. As I sniffled and wiped the tear away, Ephesia spoke and her words were not comforting.

'That's typical of you, isn't it? An innocent cat that has never done you any harm gets poisoned instead of you and do you feel sorry? Oh no. Not my husband! Not the man of the cloth! Although it should have been him lying there dead, he points out, "Luckily that cat copped it instead." And there we are. You're alive, so stuff the fact that the Lord made All Things Bright and Beautiful, because I'm alright Jack. As for Jack the Tipper? Well, *Jill the Tipper* has a tip for you. If you don't get that mess cleaned up and give that cat a decent burial the wrath of Jill will be terrible to behold.'

'But I can't clean it up. It's evidence,' I pleaded. 'The police will be here shortly. Anyone would think you cared more for a stray cat than you do for me?'

I somehow sensed this was not a hypothesis I should pursue. Fortunately, the sound of a car pulling up heralded the arrival of Glasgow's finest and remission for me.

Ephesia glared at me and hissed, 'You wait. You just wait till they go away.'

The car door slammed shut and there was a squeal of unoiled hinges as Sergeant and Poalis threw open the gate. They headed for us in a purposeful manner that announced they meant business. Sergeant fixed his gaze on Ephesia.

'Who is this?' he snapped at me.

'It's my wife,' I replied.

'No – who is this?' he demanded, pointing at Ephesia.

'It's my wife,' I repeated.

'You're kidding me on,' he said in astonishment. 'No joking – really?' he persisted.

I nodded affirmatively at him as he continued to stare at Ephesia.

With her hand outstretched Ephesia approached him. He didn't seem to realise she was offering him her hand, so transfixed was he.

'You may take my hand,' she said coquettishly. 'I don't bite.'

Sergeant looked at me for what seemed like reassurance.

'It's alright,' I assured him. 'It's only me she's angry with.'

When they shook hands I admired his professionalism in not wincing under Ephesia's firm handshake. His eyes did bulge a bit but that was only to be expected.

'And you are?' Ephesia enquired, fluttering her eyelids.

'Detective Inspector Sergeant and that's Police Constable Poalis,' he indicated to Poalis who was standing next to the dead cat about five feet to Sergeant's left.

Ephesia looked towards Poalis without taking her eyes off of Sergeant (yes – she can do that).

'So you're here to catch the bad man who is terrorising my husband. How brave you must be.'

'Not as brave as him,' said Sergeant looking at me with a small shiver and not a little sympathy. 'Now then, let's see what we have here.'

Kneeling on the path beside the dead cat, he took out a glass tube and scooped some milk into it.

'Is that evidence?' I asked.

'No,' he replied as he stood up. 'We've run short of milk down at the station. Of course, it's evidence.'

Ephesia went into peels of what I took to be laughter, although I can't swear to it as I'd never heard her do it before.

'I'll go and make us all a cup of coffee, shall I?' she trilled, flouncing off into the house. She paused at the front door. 'Or maybe you'd like something stronger?' she said, flexing her torso at Sergeant.

'No thanks,' Sergeant replied, the colour draining from his

face and inadvertently taking a step back.

We watched Ephesia disappear into the house. Poalis addressed me with a voice that was not only heavy with incredulity but also couched in polite, police jargon.

'Wath that your motht charming wife?'

'That's my only wife,' was my emphatic reply.

'If we can get back to the business in hand?' harrumphed Sergeant. 'You say there was a note pinned to the door?'

I nodded in agreement.

'How did you discover that it was there?'

'Well,' I began, 'I had just written two hymns – which, by the way, are marvellous. I think they're going to make the Church of Scotland the dominant force in world religion, really they are that good. I could let you have a copy, but quite frankly I think you'd be better waiting until they come out on a proper record. To get the full effect, you understand. I was thinking of maybe debuting in the Concert Hall, but of course that would probably be a decision for the Moderator to make. I would value your opinion nonetheless.'

Sergeant was obviously stunned with the import of what I was saying because he had a look of disbelief written all over his face. It was either that or boredom.

'However, to continue with the answer to your question, I was naturally very excited at this prospect. In fact, I almost broke into a spontaneous and – dare I say it – impromptu smile. I didn't, but my goodness it was close. Anyway, that's when the doorbell rang. Now, normally when the doorbell rings and I answer the door – well, to be absolutely accurate because I know how important accuracy is in these cases, I didn't actually *answer* the door, because of course, the door hadn't actually asked me anything – you see my point?'

Sergeant was obviously concentrating deeply because his eyes were shut and his head was resting on his chest.

'What I did, of course, was I *opened* the door. Now, as I was saying, normally when I open the door someone is usually there because obviously they've rung the bell with the intention of being there when whoever's door it is answers the d— sorry, *opens* the door. But to cut a long story short, funnily enough when I opened the door this time, lo and behold there was no one there. Now, I thought – well, OK! Maybe I imagined the whole thing – understandable, when you consider that I had just single-handedly saved my Church from potential ruin by writing the two hymns I told you about. Nevertheless, it being in my nature to leave no stone untried, I went outside to check, and that's when I noticed the note. Does that answer your question, Detective Inspector?'

'To tell you the truth,' Sergeant said, a trifle wearily I thought, 'I've forgotten what I asked.' I was about to refresh his memory when he answered hurriedly, 'But I'll live with it. I already know how the cat exited the scenario. Could you tell me – briefly – how it entered?'

Although this time his eyes did not close in concentration while he listened intently, they did glaze over as I started to relay the events appertaining to the cat's demise. It obviously was a harrowing experience for him because after I finished he turned to Poalis and sighed, 'Thank God that's over with.'

'Will you have to send the cat to the lab to find out what killed it? For what it's worth, my guess is poison,' I volunteered. Sergeant surveyed me for a moment.

'Due to the fact that there are no bullet holes, stab wounds, nylon stocking or chord marks that might have been used for strangling, tyre marks on your front doorstep that could suggest a hit-and-run, or an absence of any bruising caused by a blunt instrument, you might just have hit the nail on the head, Sherlock. Why was the cat killed? I assume we can rule out a gangland hit by a rival moggie mobster. Likewise political assassination. It could have been the old eternal triangle, but as poison looks to be the *modus operandi*, and that's never been a method used by cats to sort out their amoral disputes, this leaves us with the inescapable fact that the cat was killed by mistake, and someone in this house was the killer's true victim. As you have already been the target for malevolence, it would appear that, on the face of it, you were the intended victim and that The Tipper has upped a gear in his hatred of you.'

'I think I already knew that,' I said. 'You didn't need to string it out.'

Sergeant nodded in agreement. 'You're right. I was just getting my own back. To answer your original question, I don't think we need to wait for a lab report. The cat was poisoned by cyanide.'

'How do you know that?' I asked.

'There is a very distinct smell of almonds,' he sighed impatiently. 'To a professional who has been trained in observational techniques, the smell of almonds at the scene of a murder is a sure sign that cyanide has been used. Does that answer your question?' he asked with a smirk playing around the corners of his lips as he turned to Poalis who smiled knowingly back at him.

I nodded in agreement. 'Of course. You're right – unless someone might be baking an almond cake. I think you'll find one in Ephesia's oven,' I said, with a smirk now playing around the corners of my lips as Ephesia shouted from inside, 'Coffee's ready. Would anyone like a slice of homemade almond cake?'

'You really must try it,' I urged, as I felt a splatter of rain signalling a light shower was due. 'It'll make a nice change from all the humble pie you've had to swallow.' As I led the way into the manse I felt quite smug, despite being the target of a homicidal maniac.

Once we were seated in the living-room I gave Sergeant the note to examine. As he was studying it, Ephesia entered with a tray on which were slices of almond cake, some cups and a pot of what smelled like burnt tar – but which I knew from experience was Ephesia's attempt at coffee.

'Tell me, Mrs Jolly,' said Sergeant thoughtfully, 'did you ask the milkman to deliver an extra pint of milk?'

Ephesia shook her head and formed her mouth into what she probably thought was a pout but looked more like the spout of the coffeepot she was balancing on the tray.

'Mrs Jolly, indeed,' she scolded. 'Call me Ephesia, please. See anything you fancy?' she asked lasciviously.

'Nothing for me, thank you,' Sergeant hurriedly replied.

Shifting tack, she rounded on Poalis. 'What would you like, Constable?'

'I'm trying to watch my weight, tho' no cake, thank you. Could I have coffee without cream, pleathe?' Poalis answered.

Ephesia put the tray down on the table. 'I'm sorry, we don't have cream,' she smiled politely. 'Can you take it without milk instead?'

Poalis shook his head. 'No, I'm thorry, I don't like coffee without milk, I prefer it without cream. I can take tea without milk, though. Do you have that?'

Ephesia pondered the question. 'I'm not sure. I'll go and check for you,' she decided, heading back towards the kitchen.

Sergeant leaned over to me and whispered with a note of puzzlement in his tone. 'Is it just me or was that a totally ludicrous conversation?'

'No. It sounded fine to me,' I replied mischievously. 'Any clues from the note?' I asked, more in hope than in expectation.

'Not sure,' Sergeant said, examining the note further. 'The writing is different from the previous letters, and he has dropped The Ripper form of prose as well,' he mused, rubbing his jaw thoughtfully with his hands. 'And to tell you the truth, this shift in behavioural pattern has got to me. I'm really getting very excited. After all these years it's starting to look as though I could maybe have a proper whodunit after all.'

Before I could point out to Sergeant that no one had actually been *done* yet, Ephesia came back.

'Sorry. No can do,' she said apologetically. 'Would you like a glass of milk, though? We've got nearly two pints in the fridge.'

'Yeth thankth, if you can be bothered?' Poalis replied.

'It's no problem,' Ephesia laughed, gaily tossing her hair over her shoulder but fortunately catching it before hit the floor. 'Would you like to give me a hand?' she twittered, vanishing back into the kitchen.

'Thertainly,' said Poalis unsuspectingly, and innocently following in her footsteps. Oh dear, I thought to myself.

'Of course, at the moment we only have an *attempted* murder on our hands,' said Sergeant. 'Seeing as how it's a cat that's been done in instead of you. I'm just thinking,' he said, leaning towards me in a confidential manner, 'it might be difficult to prove in court that you were the intended victim, due to the fact that, as it was in an open situation on your doorstep, anyone could have had access to the poisoned milk. Unfortunately for us, you didn't drink it before the cat, so in law the defence might be able to argue that the cat was the intended victim all along. Damn!'

'Yes, that is unfortunate,' I agreed, with maybe a large degree of justifiable sarcasm.

Just then a scream rang through the house.

'Quick, it came from the kitchen,' Sergeant shouted, leaping to his feet and racing for the kitchen door.

I followed from a distance, fearing the worst. Ephesia could be a bit rough when her blood was up. I pulled up just behind Sergeant inside the entrance to the kitchen; my worst fears had been realised. Poalis was lying prostrate on the cold linoleum flooring, obviously unconscious. A broken glass of milk lay on the floor at his side. Over him, with her left hand clutching the neck of her blouse while the right arm steadied herself against the kitchen worktop, stood Ephesia – wide-eyed and her face fixed with a look of total astonishment.

'What happened?' said Sergeant.

I was just about to explain that Ephesia sometimes got, what you might say, carried away with the moment, when I saw that she had lifted the arm that had been supporting her and was now pointing towards the kitchen window. When my eyes settled on what she was pointing at, my breath stopped and my heartbeat did likewise.

'My God,' I heard Sergeant gasp from where he stood next to me.

Neither of us could believe our eyes for there, on the outside ledge of the kitchen window, was the dead cat – only now it was sitting up licking itself in the frankly disgusting way that cats are prone to. (Ranald used to say they looked as if they were on the phone.) It stopped what it was doing, looked at us curiously, lost interest in us and went back to its ablutions.

Sergeant took in the situation at a glance then sprang out the kitchen. I could tell from the sound of his footsteps running along the hall he was heading for the front door. I followed behind. When I got to the door he was standing scratching his head in exasperation.

'It's gone,' he gestured towards the spot beside the doorstep, which sure enough was now *sans* cat, as the French would say. I thought I'd say it as well.

'It looks as if we are *sans* cat, Detective Inspector.'

He looked round at me. 'Does that mean it's buggered off?'

I nodded in assent at his deduction, if not his choice of language.

'Damn,' he said again.

'I wonder if you could modify your language. This is a manse after all,' I requested.

He nodded absentmindedly. 'Yes, I'm sorry I said "damn",' he said.

'You said "bugger" as well,' I reminded him.

'Damn. Did I say "bugger" too?' he replied to my assertion.

'Yes, you said "damn" and "bugger".'

'Oh well, so did you,' he flung back at me.

'I would never say "damn" and "bugger",' I retorted.

'You just have,' he said, his voice rising and starting to crack a little.

'Well, yes. But only to point out to you that you had said "damn" and "bugger" first. I didn't mean to say "damn" and "bugger".'

'Neither did I, bugger it.'

I was about to point out to him that he had, in fact, used it again and this time in the form of an oath. But I could tell by the way he held his fist under my nose that he wasn't interested in pursuing this fine, theological point any longer.

By the time we had got back into the kitchen, Poalis had recovered and apologised for fainting. Sergeant and I both told him not to be silly and nobody would think any the less of him for it, while secretly thinking, what a wimp.

As Ephesia and I walked them to the front door, Sergeant consoled himself that even though they had left valuable evidence lying around on the ground which then mysteriously got up and walked away, at least he had the milk sample to analyse and hopefully that would throw some light on the situation.

We were still deep in conversation when I noticed a piece of paper jammed under the windscreen wipers of the police car. It was wet due to the light shower of rain, which had stopped now. As Sergeant removed the paper, Poalis got into the driver's seat and started up the engine. Sergeant gave the paper a cursory glance before crumpling it up, and I was waiting to see if I could catch him out as a litter lout when I noticed that his expression had changed – for the worse.

'Cut the engine, Poalis,' he ordered. As Poalis obeyed, Sergeant uncurled the piece of paper and showed me what was written on it.

> To the police
>
> No luck yet dear old boss I'm still having a jolly time watching yoo trying to catch me. Ha ha. Old miseryguts is not out of the woods yet. The cat got yoo goin – eh. Then it got itself goin ha.ha. I laffd. I do get my Jolly's watching yoo oll. But I'm throo foolin now. The tipper has been and gon. The ripper is with me now. And we're out for fun. Ha ha. Venjens is mine saith the lord. Eh? If yoo don't believe me yool be able to ask him yoorself soon. Wont that be Jolly. Jolly.
>
> Yorz in Hell. Jacky R.

Sergeant bit his bottom lip, nodded to himself as he looked around the street then snapped into action.

'Poalis, check every house, see if anyone spotted who left this on the windscreen. There must be some witnesses, try and get a description. Off you go.' Turning to Ephesia and I he added, 'This might be the break we've been looking for. So far no one has so much as caught a glimpse of him – or her, for that matter.'

'What do you mean "her"?'

I could feel the heat of Ephesia's glare on my left temporal lobe. Or, to put it another way, my ears were burning. 'What have you been up to that might make some other woman want to murder you?'

Sergeant immediately rounded on her. 'That question implied that you might want your husband dead, Mrs Jolly, and even that you might be the one who would attempt to murder him.'

Sensing he may be on to something, Sergeant probed further. 'Would you be capable of attempting to murder him?'

Ephesia's response to the question was to soften her demeanour and demurely suggest, 'Only in a husband-and-wife sort of way, Inspector.'

As Sergeant and I were trying to fathom out the meaning of Ephesia's reply and what it meant for the future of monogamy, Poalis signalled to us from across the street that the new neighbour had, in fact, seen someone at the police car.

'Tell them we'll be right over, Constable Poalis,' Sergeant shouted back. 'Before we go over there,' Sergeant said in a confidential manner, 'I want to find out what they might be like as reliable witnesses. Do you know them at all?'

'Well,' I began, 'I've only caught a glimpse of a young woman. I don't know if there is anyone else there or not. She is new to the street. But she seems quite nice.'

'In what way "nice"?' Sergeant asked.

'Nice, pert face, with blue eyes and nice, full, red lips. Nice, long blonde hair that tumbles down to her shoulders, nice slim but full figure that goes in and out nicely. She also has nice under—' I was aware that I'd maybe gone a wee bit far.

'Do continue,' was Ephesia's frosty command.

'Yes, under—, eh! under— underlay. That's right, she had new carpets delivered and I noticed that the underlay was quite, eh! stunning – more than carpet underlay usually is, in fact, I noticed that, eh! – a bit.'

'Let's go over there and see for ourselves, shall we?' Sergeant said, straightening up his tie and smoothing his hair while checking his reflection in the car wing mirrors.

'Yes. Let's,' smiled Ephesia, aiming a kick at the cruciate ligaments of my knee.

We were met at the front door by Poalis. 'Jutht to warn you, thir, the lady ith foreign and doethn't thpeek much English. Her name'th Farrit.'

Sergeant nodded, then asked, 'Is that her first name?'

Poalis shook his head. 'I don't think tho. The name on the

door ith Farrit.'

'So it is,' Sergeant affirmed after a quick glance. 'Let's find out what she saw.'

Poalis led us into the living-room. I was glad to see that the carpet fortunately looked as if it could have been new. The room was large and arranged in a fashion that I believe is called 'minimalist'. Likewise the lady of the house. She was sitting in an armchair wearing a white see-through top under which was a black see-through bra, under which was – well, you can probably guess. She was also wearing – correction, *nearly* wearing, a very small miniskirt which left very little to the imagination.

Sergeant leaned toward me and muttered into my ear, 'I see what you mean about the underlay.' Then he addressed the lady in question. 'Is it Mrs or Miss Farrit?'

'Meeses Farrit,' she said in what sounded to me like a strong mid-European accent.

She pointed to her wedding ring, as if to help explain. 'I yam wee doh?'

'Och,' I said, 'you're not that wee, especially if you put on stiletto heels and black fishnet stocki—'

Sergeant nudged me. 'I think Mrs Farrit is telling us she is a widow.'

She smiled in acknowledgement.

'Thank you, Mrs Farrit.' Sergeant went on to introduce everyone and then asked her for her first name so they were up to scratch with the formalities. She nodded in understanding and tapped her hand on her breastbone.

'Gaghin. My name, yes?'

Sergeant signalled he understood and said to Poalis, 'Get that down in your notebook, Poalis. The lady is a widow and she's Gaghin Farrit.'

Poalis assented that was the case.

'Could you tell us what you saw?'

With hand gestures that signified she was looking for words, she slowly and laboriously related to us that she had seen a figure standing beside the police car and they had put something under the windscreen wipers. And yes, she had got a good look. This obviously raised our expectations of a description. Yes, she could see that it was a man. He had on a tartan tammy through which thick, rather dry, lifeless and long ginger hair stuck out. He had a bulbous, red nose and was dressed in a candy-striped pullover with large baggy trousers, and she noticed he also had abnormally large feet.

'I've got all that down, thir,' said Poalis as he intently finished writing in his notebook.

'It looks like we're looking for some clown with a 'See You Jimmy' wig on. Is that right?' Sergeant said sarcastically.

'Yeth, thir. Thyould be eathy enough to thpot, thir.'

'Tell me, Mrs Farrit. Did he make his escape in a wee motorcar that fell apart as it went round and round in a circle?' said Sergeant, performing a most elaborate mime.

Mrs Farrit shook her head. 'No. No – he ryyde away on a bisexual.' I admit I reddened visibly.

Sergeant gasped, 'A bi-sexual. How could you tell?'

Mrs Farrit nodded to let us know she had understood the question. 'Becaas,' she said, 'he ding-a-lingd on thee – haow yoo sayee? – andelbaar, I theenk, no?'

We all sighed with relief. 'For a minute there I thought we were in trouble,' Sergeant exclaimed. 'Let's rap up here. I don't think we're going any further with this one.'

'Thyall I put out an all pointth bulletin for the thuthpect, thir,' said you know who.

'Well, it's an unusual way to hand in your resignation, but go ahead, why not? Frankly, I'm at that stage of the investigation where I don't give an aperture on a monkey's anus,' said Sergeant.

Walking over to Mrs Farrit, he offered his hand. 'Please don't get up,' he said, staring down her cleavage. 'May I ask how your husband died?'

'Af coorse. My hoosband – hee died on thee job.'

Noticing that my mouth was hanging open in a not-very-attractive way, Sergeant kindly lifted my jaw up with a cursory movement of his right hand as he passed me on the way out.

'An accident at work, I take it, Mrs Farrit?' he offered by way of an explanation.

She shrugged her shoulders in a fatalistic gesture.

'Right! We're off, then. We'll let ourselves out.'

Making our way to the door we noticed that Ephesia was on her knees. She had prised the fitted carpet off the wall and as we passed she grunted, 'As underlays go, I don't think it's anything special.'

W HEN WE GOT BACK OUTSIDE I asked Sergeant about the clown outfit and the 'See You Jimmy' wig. He explained it was obviously a disguise and that the culprit had probably cycled round the corner to a waiting van and bundled the bike and the disguise inside. This proved to be the case. Quite a few witnesses said they saw a clown figure despatching notes under the windscreen wipers of cars in the street, but assumed it was just a promotional gimmick. And on inspection, all the notes proved to be blank. No one unfortunately saw a van, but it seemed logical that that was how the fiend made his escape.

Sergeant suggested we call it a day as there was not much chance of further developments. I was feeling a bit apprehensive about being alone with a vengeful Ephesia, but she must have been tired as well because when we got back inside the manse she let me off with a glare.

For the next few days things calmed down, thank the Lord, and I took the opportunity to just wander around pretty aimlessly. I even took time to give Ranald a hand to select a suitable spot for burial. We finally found a spot he liked, but he said he would like to try it out before committing himself. So I left him as he lay down on the favoured spot for the night.

The next morning he came to the manse bright and early full of enthusiasm for his choice. It was just what he had always been looking for, he enthused, and went on about how it was the best night's sleep he'd had in ages. As he left skipping down the road, I hadn't the heart to tell him that when it came to purchasing his dream grave, the fact that it was the lay-by of the Kingston Bridge motorway was likely to prove a stumbling block.

As Ranald left, the postie delivered the mail. I had just finished making a cup of tea for myself (Ephesia was having a long lie in) and when I picked up the mail my heart skipped a beat. There on one of the letters was the unmistakable mark of the

Church of Scotland.

I carried it through to my desk and with the cup of tea at my side I sat down, thrilled at the prospect of reading the congratulatory commendations regarding my updating of the hymns.

```
Jolly
We note that you did not reply as to the
allegations of drug-taking made against you. I
must admit this puzzled me as I thought that
even you would want to refute such a charge.

   However, all became clear when I opened a
letter with your suggestions of how to improve
on our beloved Church hymns. Also the change
of text you supplied to us.

   While it is true that we are looking at ways
towards making the words of our old faithfuls
more appropriate to a modern society, we have
not yet gone completely doo-lally, unlike you.

   The contents of the letter were obviously
the product of a drug-ravaged mind. We as a
body will offer you every assistance to return
to planet Earth, however in the meantime we
cannot allow you to continue to preach to the
members of our Church - even though there are
only two of them - while you are obviously as
high as a kite. We therefore, as responsible
representatives of the Church, must ask you to
accept one month's notice.

   I am deeply sorry
Yours
```

Simpson Simmons

SIMPSON SIMMONS
ASSISTANT TO NIVEN SIMMONS AND WILSON SIMMONS,
BUT AGAIN, STRANGELY, NO RELATION

I confess I felt nothing as the cup fell from my grasp, the breath from my body escaped in gasps and for the first time in my life I experienced what it feels like to be truly alone. My Church had been my life, but now I was to have it taken from me. Not even the chance to build up the congregation was open to me. A door had been slammed shut on my heart and for the life of me I didn't know what I had done to deserve it.

The Tipper or Ripper had done his work well. He had ripped away my spirit. All hope and reason to be alive drained from my being as I sat in my favourite old chair and sobbed. Why was God punishing me so? I was maybe not the best minister who had ever served Him, but I had done my best. I could do no more. If it was His will that I should no longer serve Him as a minister of the Church, then so be it. I would accept it as His will. And in my heart I knew that I would also continue to serve Him, in my own way, the best that I could for I knew no other way. The Ripper could not take that from me.

I decided not to tell Ephesia for the moment – maybe not even for the month. I would pick a time when I thought it appropriate, not to mention safe.

As I sat in my old chair meditating, the phone rang. It was Sergeant; his voice was strangely comforting.

'I thought you'd be interested to know that we've traced the substances that were in the milk,' he said. 'As you pointed out, it was not cyanide. It was curare, a drug used by the natives of South America.' He paused while I took in what he had related. 'I didn't know much about curare – it being one of the few drugs that the natives of Glasgow don't sell outside the discotheques at the weekend – so I delved into its background and found out that the Indians used it on the tips of their arrows to knock down monkeys from the treetops when they were hunting.'

'I never knew monkeys hunted,' I said incredulously.

'No, not the monkeys,' he said, after a pause. 'The natives

171

hunted. They used the curare on the monkeys.'

'So why did he use it on a cat and not a monkey?' I asked.

'Well, there are not a lot of monkeys round these parts, are there?' He sounded tense as he continued. 'What intrigued me was that I found out that curare doesn't kill the monkey, it paralyses it. That means the meat will remain fresh until they decide to have their Sunday joint, and it also means that The Ripper – as he now wants to be known – wanted you alive, but unconscious.'

'Why?' I asked, my brain whirling with the assault it had been forced to endure in the last ten minutes.

Sergeant let out a long, slow breath. 'I think The Ripper wanted to play with you.'

'But I haven't played with anyone since I was a wee boy,' I said.

For the first time I realised Sergeant must have been religious himself when I heard him quietly say, 'Dear God in Heaven, help me with this man.' His voice came back to its previous level and he said, 'I meant *toy* with you. Like a cat would play with a mouse.'

'With a mouse,' I echoed knowingly. 'Of course, because there are no monkeys for the cat to play with round here. Yes! I see what you're getting at.'

There was a long pause. 'I wonder if you would just listen for a while?' he said at last. 'It would help me concentrate. I have an idea germinating in my head. At the moment it's only a hunch – a notion, but it won't go away. Of course, I need to do some more investigating, but fingers crossed I think at last I may be on to something.'

The phone went dead. I took it as a sign that he had hung up. Mind you, the way things were going for me it was probably the telephone company cutting me off.

Although Sergeant's phone call was trying to give me consolation of some sort, I still felt puzzled and absolutely at a loss. I was reminded of the story of the vexed Apostle.

'Master', he said, 'I am vexed and troubled in my heart, for I would know what drives men to sin.'

The Master considered his troubled friend and said, 'What makes a grain of sand mightier than an army? Will not the beggar be more merciful than a thousand merchants? And if an apple falls from an orange tree, will the pomegranate weep? Verily, I say unto you, these things are true and for all time.'

'I understand now,' said the Apostle.

'Really? I wish I did,' said the Master.

I smiled to myself. If *he* could be mystified, then why was I worried? Once again I had been shown that in the eyes of the Lord I was merely a man, as we all were: father, Ranald, me, mother, Ephesia, we were all men in the Lord's eyes – Ephesia probably that bit more.

The phone rang again. At least I knew I hadn't been cut off, which was small consolation.

'Hullo.' I sounded miserably enthusiastic, if that's possible. A low chuckle sounded through the receiver. 'Who is this?'

'It's me.' The voice was harsh and loaded with menace. 'Your old pal Jolly Jack. You don't know what Oi looks like, but Oi wants you to remember moy voice when you'se troy to sleep tonight.' The fiend started to chortle; his accent was sort of West Country and his laugh was like a firework, crackling and sparking and fizzing around my ears.

'What have I ever done to you that's made me your enemy? I don't even know you.' My own voice was breaking up with fear.

'Shut up, you sanctimonious piece of blubber. You'll knows me soon enough alright.' Again the laugh, this time hissing as though through gritted teeth, almost like gas escaping. 'Oi'll pay you back, Jolly, and Oi'll laugh when you whine for mercy. I hate it when you whine. Whine. Whine. Whine.' His voice tailed away to a malicious whisper. 'While you whine, Oi'll

173

laugh. Ha. Ha. Ha. Boye boye. Tara fit now.' And for the second time the phone went dead.

I phoned Sergeant immediately. The receiver at the other end was taken up, also immediately.

'I want to speak to Detective Inspector Sergeant,' I panted. 'I must speak to him right away. Please, it's very important. Please.'

A voice answered me. 'I know it's important, Jolly. The Ripper's been on to you, hasn't he?'

'How do you know? Who is this?'

'It's me, Sergeant, and I know because I put a bug on your line. We've taped the conversation. I'm coming over. Don't leave the manse.'

I was not going to leave the chair, never mind the manse. A tiny mouse squealed and ran along the skirting for cover. A sure sign Ephesia was up and about.

I HEARD THE LIVING-ROOM DOOR OPEN and Ephesia's voice announcing, 'He'll be in here.' After a pause she boomed, 'Jolly, come out from behind the armchair. Detective Inspector Sergeant's here. He wants to question you, not play hide-and-seek. Remember, Detective! If you want to inspect anything, you only have to ask.'

The audible sigh of relief escaping from Sergeant's oesophagus led me to believe Ephesia had left and we were alone.

'You alright?' Sergeant's voice contained an unfamiliar note of concern.

'Yes, thank you.' My voice contained an all-*too*-familiar note of concern.

'You really can come out from behind the chair, you know,' Sergeant said coaxingly.

'OK! I trust you,' I said, rising to my feet but staying behind my favourite chair.

'What a nice teddy bear you're hugging. Yours?' he asked, the note of concern now in his eyes as well as his voice.

'Yes,' I laughed nervously while bouncing Teddy on my knees. 'I used to be dependent on a dreadful old comfort blanket, but thankfully I grew out of that.'

He nodded understandingly. 'Well, you do don't you. Mind if I sit down?'

I gestured to the chair nearest to me. It was fairly comfortable but more importantly it made sure that he was between me and anyone coming bursting in through the door.

He removed his coat and sat down. He was studying me while at the same time affecting a smile that tried to say, I'm not studying you, honest I'm not. I smiled back with a smile that tried to say, thank goodness I'm so normal that you're not studying me.

After a moment or two of deliberation, he leaned back in his chair, took a deep breath and seemed to make up his mind.

'Reverend Jolly, I'm going to be very straight with you and try to lay out what I feel about this, eh, shall we say, unfortunate situation you find yourself in.'

I cuddled Teddy tighter to me, which seemed to help.

'I can see that you're a man of – what's the best way to put this?' His eyes swept over Teddy and I. 'Unusual courage – yes, I think that's a fair description. I want to tell you up front my assessment of the situation so far, and more importantly how we can bring it to an end and try to avoid you getting murdered.'

Teddy leapt up from my knees and threw his arms around my neck. He was also shaking uncontrollably.

Sergeant gazed at him and then said concernedly, 'Is, eh, he going to be alright, do you think?'

I nodded my head firmly. 'Oh yes.' My head would not stop nodding. 'He'll be fine, as long as I'm with him.'

Sergeant seemed relieved. 'Good. It's lucky for him you're there!'

I swallowed hard. 'Oh! I can't take all the credit. It's a two-way thing. He might even want to whine and lose control of his bodily functions. Sometimes I do all that for him, just so he won't look pathetic, you understand.'

Sergeant took another deep breath. 'Sure. Tell you what,' he continued – I noticed his head was now nodding a lot as well – 'if he looks like he might, eh, lose control of his bodily functions, would you let me know? I could then leave the room and save him the embarrassment of me having to smell his bodily functions. Hmm! What do you think?'

'Eh, yes,' I agreed. 'As long as you don't go away and leave him in the manse on his own.'

'Wouldn't dream of it,' Sergeant replied in agreement. 'OK. Down to business. For what it's worth, I don't think that you are in danger of being murdered. I think the so-called Ripper does not have it in him to go that far. I can't be sure, of course, but that's my educated guess. By the way, let me apologise for bugging your phone – I should have asked your permission, but you may just have betrayed the fact the call was being taped if you'd been aware that there was a bug on the phone. Before you ask, a bug does not mean an insect, it's police slang for allowing us to hear a private conversation.'

'Please, Inspector, give me credit. I'm not that stupid,' I lied.

Ignoring me, he carried on. 'I listened to the tape on the road here via the car tape-deck and not once does he actually threaten physical violence. It's all to do with psychological torture – for example, how he's going to enjoy listening to you whine; how he wants you to lie awake thinking of his voice. It sounds to me as if he does not possess the nerve to confront his inadequacies. So, in order to carry on in his wish to terrify you, he has adopted the persona of Jack the Ripper, thereby transferring his emotions away from him on to someone who's not even living. That way he does not have to accept the responsibility for his lack of courage.'

'It sounds sick to me,' I said, giving Teddy a reassuring hug. 'What else have you deduced?' I asked, beginning to feel a fascination that was at least stopping Teddy from getting more frightened.

'He has provided us with more than a psychological profile. We also know one more thing from the tape.' He paused – I sensed for effect. I also sensed he was not going to volunteer the information unless I played along.

'What do we – I mean, you know?' I said inevitably.

'That he is – male. So far we have been merely *assuming* that it was a man we were dealing with. Now we know for certain. I ran it through a voice digitaliser and there can be no doubt, he's male alright. Unfortunately, that is as far as we can go. I have no idea *who* the creep actually is. To stand any chance of finding him I would need to know every single male you had met or had dealings with recently, and that would require a feat of memory that is beyond anyone but a trained memory expert. However, let's be positive. I want you to write down for me as much as you can remember of acquaintances, people you've had dealings with etcetera – a tall order, I know, but do your best.'

I may have imagined it, but it seemed to me that Teddy gave a sigh of relief. Certainly his grip around my neck slackened off.

'I may be of more help than you think, Inspector.' He looked at me quizzically. 'You see, circumstances have dictated that I keep a journal of all that has happened to me for some considerable time. It's an extremely full account of everyone I have met, written to, and indeed had any meaningful dealings with recently. Would you like me to give it to you?'

Sergeant's face visibly shone and his cheeks rose up on either side of his nose in what I can only describe as a very broad grin. As he rose to his feet, he crossed over, shook my hand, patted Teddy on the head and said, 'In the words of a well-known commercial, "That'll do nicely".'

As I went to get the journal I stopped and, turning to him, said in a quiet tone, 'I need hardly add you will treat the contents in the strictest confidence.' I raised a finger to my lips and then tapped on the side of my nose in the age-old sign that we shared a secret. He rolled one trouser leg up, undid his shirt and bared one of his breasts in an even older sign that we shared a secret. I handed the journal over to him and we shook hands for quite a long time before he left. I felt instinctively that he and I were on the same side at last. I have, of course, written this last bit after he returned the journal, and I now await with no small degree of optimism that he will be able to rid me of you know who.

Teddy awaits also.

THIS MORNING I've been on tenterhooks waiting to find out if Sergeant has got any nearer to finding the identity of my tormentor. Finally I decided that, whatever the outcome, Ephesia and I deserved a holiday – nothing special, just a wee relaxing break. Unfortunately, I phoned the railway company. After about twenty-five minutes talking in circles to a machine, I finally got through to a human. I have it on tape due to the police still monitoring my calls. They sent me the following transcript:

RAIL PERSON: You're through to ticket sales. How can I help?

ME: I'd like two returns to Pitlochry, please.

RAIL PERSON: Uh hu! Do you want a cheap-day return, an economy return, an away-day special return, a half-day special return, a midweek tourist all-inclusive winter-week special return, an out-and-about all-inclusive special weekday cheap-rate exclusive to weekend-travellers-arriving-at-6.30 a.m.-and-leaving-at-9 p.m.-on-a-Tuesday-only return?

ME: Eh! I'm not quite sure. I wonder, could you tell me?

RAIL PERSON: I only sell tickets. Passenger enquiries are at 0141–

ME: Wait a minute, don't go. I've been on the line for twenty-five minutes, I don't want to lose my place. Just an ordinary return will do.

RAIL PERSON: An ordinary return? Are you trying to be funny?

ME: No, of course not.

RAIL PERSON: We only do specials that attract more customers, therefore making it cheaper and so passing on the benefits to ill-informed people like you, sir.

ME: Oh! I see, thanks.

RAIL PERSON: No problem. We're trained to handle the intellectually challenged. Or to use your official title, 'passengers'. Thank you for calling, caller –

ME: Wait. Don't go. I'll have the, eh! – eh! –

RAIL PERSON: Yes.

ME: The third one.

RAIL PERSON: The midweek tourist all-inclusive winter-week special?

ME: Yes.

RAIL PERSON: You cannae have that.

ME: Eh?

RAIL PERSON: There isn't an 'r' in the month, is there? They're only available when there's an 'r' in the month. Dear God. What are yez like? It's fully explained in the *Helpful Hints and Information on Tickets* booklet.

ME: Right, I see, where can I get one of them?

RAIL PERSON: Oh! They're no' for you – they're for us. We need them in order for us to help you find the correct ticket, at the right price. Don't we?

ME: Well, in that case could you find me one?

RAIL PERSON: I've already told you all about them. I cannot make your mind up for you, sir. I have other people to help.

ME: If you could just tell me the difference in price between a special and an economy.

RAIL PERSON: The special is fifteen pounds dearer.

ME: Why is that?

RAIL PERSON: What is this, *University Challenge*? You get a free cup of tea and a biscuit with the special, OK? But I'll warn you, that's only for a limited period, it goes up next week.

ME: Alright. I'll take two specials.

RAIL PERSON: Right. Do you want to sit down during the journey?

ME: If that's alright.

RAIL PERSON: I'll make an appointment with seat reservations for you.

ME: Eh! I don't know if I'll have time to –

RAIL PERSON: Three weeks on Wednesday, 10.30 a.m. The earliest I can do for you. Don't tell me, let me guess. That'll no' suit you, will it?

ME: Well! No, it won't.

RAIL PERSON: No! It never does. Yez all expect to just walk into a station and there's all these trains lying about, wi' seats, just waiting to whisk you all off on a carefree journey while you sit back drinking tea and alcohol and eatin' three-course meals and havin' your bags carried so that you arrive there all fresh and raring to go, just like in the adverts. That *is* what yez expect. Go on, admit it, don't you?

ME: Well. Yes. That would be very nice.

RAIL PERSON: Oh! Wouldn't it just. It would also be nice if we lived in a world without war and poverty, and if I looked like Brad Pitt and could take free kicks like David Beckham, but we don't, do we, sir? And because we're forced to print timetables, yez expect us to keep to them? And of course, when the company leaves you stranded on a pissing wet night and you're soaked to the skin, that'll be our fault as well, eh?

ME: Eh, I wonder if I could speak to the machine again?

RANALD TURNED UP TODAY, very downcast. He had been to the city planning department to lodge a claim in his preferred choice of The Kingston Bridge motorway for his 'final sleep-over', as father insisted on calling Ranald's eventual demise. As I feared, they had turned down his application on the grounds that it would disrupt traffic. Ranald seemed inconsolable, so as usual it fell to me to raise his spirits and try and put a positive spin on his predicament.

Even I was finding it difficult to find a bright side till it dawned on me that the Kingston Bridge motorway was:

(a) a motorway and

(b) a bridge

and, of course, being a bridge meant that it went over water – which in this case was the River Clyde.

'So, what's your point?' said Ranald moodily as he tried in vain to lick his left nostril with his tongue. He of course failed and this seemed to put him into an even fouler mood.

'My point is . . .' I stopped because Ranald was now holding his nostril between his thumb and forefinger and was – for want of a better description – tugging and hauling viciously at it while squealing with pain. 'What are you doing?' I cried out.

Tears of frustration were pouring down his cheek as the act of tugging and pulling at his nostril was dragging him round the room. 'If thy left nostril offend thee then pluck it out,' he shouted, misquoting Matthew 5 verse 28.

I finally caught him when he got himself entangled in the leaves of an overgrown Swiss cheese plant that had taken over a shady area of the living-room that was inclined to damp rot.

Pinning his arms to his side, I yelled into his left ear, 'You've got it wrong. It's not your left nostril. It's your right eye.'

With a cry of bewilderment that rent my heart asunder, he shouted back, 'Impossible! No one can lick their right eye with their tongue.' Then, with a simple nod of acceptance, he wiped his tears away, apologised to the Swiss cheese plant and asked,

'So, what's your point about the bridge over the River Clyde?'

'OK. Now, don't reject this out of hand,' I soothed. 'Although your first choice of a burial spot on the lay-by of the bridge would, on the face of it, appear to be dead in the water, carry that thought on a bit.'

His eyes registered interest while his nose registered pain. Then his face lit up as he started to twig what I was suggesting.

'Of course!' he yelled. 'I could be dropped over the side of the bridge into the Clyde. That way I would at least be near by my lay-by.' Hugging me with both arms, he danced me round the room. 'You're a genius.' He was crying in unbridled delight as he started kissing me.

Ephesia entered, took in the scene and exclaimed, 'What did I say about him? I was right, wasn't I?' I assumed she was referring to Ranald, then I noticed she was pointing at me while talking to Detective Inspector Sergeant. 'I'll leave you to it, Inspector.' She gave me a withering look as she closed the door and I just heard the word 'degenerate' as the door slammed shut.

Sergeant stood awkwardly, shuffling from side to side and biting his lip in the mannerism I now knew he adopted when he was nervous. In an attempt to break the ice, I peeled Ranald from my body and introduced him to Sergeant.

'This is my brother Ranald.'

I saw the look of horror on Sergeant's face as he repeated my declaration, '*Your brother?*'

'There's nothing like that I assure you, Detective Inspector,' I hastily added. 'Ranald's just had good news and he got a bit excited, that's all.'

Sergeant relaxed. 'Oh, right. My mistake.' He smiled forgivingly. 'What's the good news then?'

'I'm going to be thrown into the Clyde when I finally get to die,' Ranald announced, his face flushed with excitement.

I noticed that Sergeant had begun to bite his lip again. 'Could

I perhaps have a word with you in private, Reverend Jolly?' he suggested.

After I had assured Ranald that the police were not going to ban his death plunge from the Kingston Bridge, he agreed to take his leave and with one last kiss and hug he left singing:

The River Clyde, the wonderful Clyde,

The sound of it thrills me and fills me with pride.

I'm satisfied what e'er may betide

I'm going to be buried at the bottom of the Clyde.

Sergeant didn't say much until the door had slammed shut. Then, after a moment's deliberation, he asked, 'Just the two of you in the family then?'

'Yes!' I nodded, filling in an awkward pause. 'Ranald's my younger brother.'

After another long pause during which Sergeant seemed to be wrestling with an uneasy decision, eventually he seemed to come to a conclusion.

'Normally,' he deliberated, 'we wouldn't allow someone to be thrown off the Kingston Bridge lay-by, however in his case,' he said, more to himself than me, 'I think we'll make an exception.'

'Oh! That is good news!' I exclaimed, marvelling again at how Ranald's infectious enthusiasm had ensnared even a hard-bitten policeman in its charm.

'That is not what I wanted to talk to you in private about, however.' He looked around awkwardly. I realised that I had forgotten my manners and motioned him to sit down.

He pulled up a chair and seemed to want me to do likewise.

Waiting until I had sat in my favourite chair, he gave me a lengthy, enquiring look which I don't mind admitting unnerved me somewhat.

'I had, as you know, a copy made of the journal you provided me with. I studied it over and over and I don't mind telling you, was beginning to lose hope and then . . .' He paused, as though gathering his thoughts. 'I began to get a faint glimmer, a chink of light shone through, and gradually it started to seem as if I might just have this fiend in my sights. I was about fifty–fifty as to his identity but I couldn't get the proof I needed. This morning, however, this arrived.'

He passed over what looked like another note. I gave him a questioning glance.

'Yes,' he stated with a shrug. 'It's from our friend.'

Tentatively I started to read:

Dear Boss
  It's me agen Yoor old frend Jacky boy. I do laff at yoor trying to find me. Still haven't a clue ave yoo? Yoo shood ave, becos I gave you a good one last time. Too late now though eh. Ha Ha Ha. Old miseryguts looks like he's goin to crack up any time now.
  If yoo can't catch me. He's done fer. And yoo can't, can yoo. Ha Ha Ha.
  From Hell
  Jack

I shook my head disconsolately. 'He's right, you know. I am starting to crack up.'

Sergeant studied the floor for a moment then, looking up, he said, 'At last he's made a mistake. I think I've got him – I think I know his identity.'

He could see my eyes light up with a mixture of expectation, hope and a longing that soon my torment would be at an end.

'If I can get everyone who you've recently rubbed up the wrong way under one roof for questioning, then I'm fairly positive I can bring this case to an end. Unfortunately the police station is not big enough to hold all the suspects at the same time. I want to use the church to make the final deductions, which hopefully will lead to his arrest. I need your permission. Do I have it?' At that precise moment he could have had my hand in marriage. 'I'll take that look as a yes.'

He got up and crossed to the door. 'Fingers crossed, this Sunday we'll get him.'

UNDAY. It's been five days since Sergeant offered me the prospect of a way out of this nightmare that I'm caught up in and now it's arrived. It's so strange. Normally I have prepared a sermon but as I only have two of a flock and they're both normally asleep I'm hardly, as they say, under pressure.

It's a grey, rain-flecked morning. Seagulls are hovering overhead signalling stormy weather, two magpies are bullying their smaller neighbours and, to continue with the bird scenario, I would rather like to duck out of attending church for the first time in my life.

Today, however, I may finally find out who has made my life a misery and why.

Ephesia has been magnificent. Now that she realises the strain I've been under she has been an absolute tower of strength, going so far as to give up her SAS circuit training, thus putting in jeopardy her chances of winning this year's World's Strongest Lollipop Woman title. She has done all that just so she can act as bodyguard for me when we leave to go to Church.

I hesitate to criticise when she has been so wonderful towards me, but I do think tying loose branches to her camouflage outfit, blacking her cheeks and crawling along the ground on her elbows is maybe carrying out her responsibilities a bit too far. What is normally a fifteen-minute walk to Church took an hour and ten minutes due to Ephesia's travel arrangements, but we finally got there without a sniper's bullet finding its mark, so who am I to criticise her thoroughness?

Once inside I felt more at ease and had a chance to take stock of proceedings. Sergeant informed me that he had instructed anyone who he felt bore me a grudge to appear. I was, as I say, apprehensive that I might have to confront the one or two people on Sergeant's list.

I was surprised to see Lorna Maclumpha and Peaches McGuffie sat there. Just because I had unwittingly varnished

187

them both to a pew I could not see that as justification for putting me through Hell. Still, they were glaring at me so who knows. Also glaring at me was the porridge-swallower and indeed all of the spiritualists from Ephesia's psychic meeting. Next to them a high court judge, a scoutmaster and a chief constable were wedged in besides a Lifeboys captain, an American priest and the entire cast of *The Mousetrap*. Just behind them were Virago, Madonna and baby Britney, who were deep in conversation with the unhappy burial party I had passed while singing 'There is a happy land, far, far away'. The waiters from our favourite restaurant were comparing notes with the paperboy, the postman and the crew of the refuse collection squad. There was also a sizeable proportion of the Hum A Hymn auditionees mixing with Bridget Hegarty and her eight children, who obviously still harboured resentment about the mistaken Lotto win affair. My two dowdy but faithful parishioners, Ava Rishious and Ann Gostura, were boring the shapely behind off the lovely Mrs Gaghin Farrit, while to her left Virginia and her husband were still telling everyone that, not only had I tried to drown their child but that I had then thrown the baby at its father. Her drug-obsessed firebrand of a brother-in-law Frankie was swathed in bandages and trying to light an extremely long cigarette through an available slit in his facial swathing. Sitting in front of them were Ephesia, mother, father and Ranald. Next to them sat two prison governors, Poalis, old Mr Crabbit, R. Sinparsley and Mr Majid.

Ephesia was annoyed because father persisted in trying to see if he could set her camouflage alight. Father was annoyed because Frankie the Firebrand kept nudging him in the back, giving him the thumbs up, offering him a draw of his cigarette and inviting him to some meeting behind the bookie's at seven o' clock, while Frankie was annoyed because Ranald – mistaking him for a real mummy – kept asking him for his autograph. It was the liveliest I had ever seen my wee church.

Then a whistle sounded and its shrill note brought silence to the proceedings. Sergeant walked from the back of the church. His gait was unhurried and measured, almost as if he were giving everyone time to assimilate his character. His head glanced from side to side occasionally, making sure he had taken in everyone who was there, and also making sure they had noted how composed and most of all how confident he looked. I entertained the thought that I was glad I was not the one who he intended exposing, but then I never was one for exposing myself.

As he climbed the steps to the pulpit, his footsteps echoed through the church and drew attention to his presence which, when he reached the top, seemed to fill the pulpit, and I had no doubt that every eye was fully concentrated on him and him alone. He began to speak. His voice was strong and resonant.

'I would like to outline what we are here for. The Reverend I. M. Jolly, minister of this church, has been subjected to as savage and vicious a series of threats as I personally have ever encountered. It has resulted in him being harassed to a point where he has been reduced to acting like a snivelling, pathetic excuse for manhood, with no pride in himself, no sense of worth, blubbering and whining and indulging in emotions that no real man would ever countenance.'

Well, thank you, I thought, as I saw every face in the throng survey me with contempt.

'But,' he continued, 'note I said that he *acted* this way. Because that is what he was doing – *acting*. That will be a description we will use more than once before we unmask the pest who tried to unsettle the Reverend I. M. Jolly. And that's all that the perpetrator of these threats was – a pest. Never once did he penetrate the iron grip of courage that this man – this giant called Jolly – carries around him like a shield. His only thought when he came to seek my help was for his parishioners, his flock. "*I don't care about me.*" That's what he said to me when he

189

stood, like a Colossus, in my office. *"I want this pest brought to justice in case he infects my flock."*

'I must admit I was sceptical that this deceptively long streak of apparent abject misery could show the courage that was needed to forge the way through to the very end. I need never have feared. This is a man who walks with gods. This is Prince Valiant, Moses and General George Patton rolled into one compact fighting-machine. This is what the *pest* tried to bring down with a few cringe-making letters. Before I go any further, are there any questions?'

All I could see were faces with their mouths wide open turned to me in incomprehension. I glanced at my reflection in a window; my mouth was open too. Old Crabbit put up his hand.

'Yes, you have a question, Mr Crabbit?' asked Sergeant.

'Will there be a collection?' asked Crabbit, as he stood up.

'No,' said Sergeant.

'Good,' said Crabbit as he sat back down again to a sigh of relief from the congregation.

They turned once more to me with what I can only describe as an expression of admiration glowing from their normally dull, tedious and torporous faces. I wished Sergeant would carry on telling them how wonderful I was. But he never.

'I am not here, though, to tell you all what you probably knew already. I'm here to unmask the pestilence that dared to try to upset your minister.' A low growl went round the flock. 'That's right, this pimple – this little piece of snot on the nostril of humanity – is sitting among you now. He came along here tonight thinking he was safe, that no one could unmask him, because this piffling little trifle of a man thought he could match wits with I. M. Jolly.'

The crowd started to snigger and a few voices could be heard saying, 'Imagine trying to match the minister.' 'Aye, must be a total tube, whoever he is.' 'Well, it wouldn't be me.'

'Nor me neither.'

I nodded modestly to my new admirers – and even winked at some of them, who were signalling to ask if I would give them an autograph.

Sergeant's whistle once again brought them to order. He surveyed them all, letting his gaze rest on certain individuals. He was now definitely toying with his adversary.

'And now I will tell you who this cowardly cretin is. By a process of elimination and good old-fashioned police leg work, I have tracked him down and even,' he chuckled to himself, 'persuaded the dumb cluck to turn up at his own identification parade.'

The crowd again joined in with his mocking grin.

'Let's consider some suspects. There's old Mr Crabbit; he undoubtedly hates the minister. He's made no secret of it, so he has a reason to want to see him suffer.' Old Crabbit's eyes darted furtively, while his face screwed itself into a snarl. 'But then he hates everybody, so he would find it impossible to narrow it down to just the one individual. No, it ain't him.' Crabbit's face unfurled from the snarl to his normal expression of mere distaste.

'What about R. Sinparsley? Could he be a prospective Sweeney Todd? Again, he has all the sadistic tendencies that are required, he likes the sight of blood, and again, he does not like the minister. But what could he have as a possible motive?'

Sinparsley leapt to his feet. 'He stole a *Daily Record* from my shop, and I think it was him that took *The Sun* as well,' he shouted out. 'What more do you want?'

Sergeant shook his head. 'No. Ladies and gents, as he has just demonstrated, he's too stupid.' Murmurs of agreement rippled round the church. 'Too stupid to carry out a calculated campaign that would result in the destruction of this fine man you see before you.'

Voices could be heard concurring: 'Thick as a plank!' 'I think he's too stupid even to cut hair.' 'You might have a point there.'

'His wife Ephesia? She would argue that she has motive enough, but when you see them together you can only come to the conclusion they deserve each other, and she would find it well nigh impossible to find anyone else in the entire universe that would be as suitable for her. And the same for him.'

I must admit a lump came to my throat when I heard that as the 'Awwws!' went round the church. Ephesia blew a kiss, and also blew the wig off a prison governor sat in front.

'Also, our culprit is a man – we know that for sure. Which brings me to the Reverend's own family. His father is a man given to unusual foibles and strange hobbies. He's more than capable of the type of mental torture inflicted by our self-styled Jack the Ripper. He's also shown that the fact that the victim was his own son would not be a drawback as all his life he has enjoyed annoying anyone, including members of his own family. Indeed, he lists it among his hobbies. He also loves to plot and plan and sees everyone else as mere fodder for his machinations.'

'*Bingo!*' shouted my mother. 'Got him in one.'

Sergeant smiled as he saw my mother go back to sleep before my father could upbraid her.

'Yes, I seriously considered the father, but then I remembered we had found a note in the church roof and there could be no way that Mr Jolly Senior could have got up there at his age.'

A huge sigh of relief escaped from my lips that he had discounted father.

'Then I remembered Jolly Jnr,' he went on, 'R. U. Jolly 2, that is. He's certainly young enough to climb up to the church roof, and he's in awe of his father – always willing to do Daddy's bidding.'

His gaze landed unflinchingly on Ranald, who gazed unflinchingly back at him. 'Of course, it couldn't be Ranald, though, because he is too caught up in his own downfall to worry about anyone else's.'

He stroked his chin, wrapped up in his thoughts. 'Our culprit has, what we'll call, a personality. We all have one, of course, and it's impossible to suppress it – not for any serious length of time anyway. But remember what I said earlier about the description 'actor'. Now, an actor *is* able to suppress his personality for long periods of time – in fact, that's what they do best, that's when an actor is most comfortable, when they can live in the skin of someone other than their true self. You'll often hear an actor say that he doesn't know who or what his real self is. And that is what our man is – an *actor*.

'When I considered all the clues and then fitted the psychological profile, I was left in no doubt that our so-called "Jack the Ripper" could only be one person.'

His gaze travelled to where the cast of *The Mousetrap* were sitting. 'And that is, of course, *you!*'

His finger pointed to the first member of the cast, then travelled across the remainder to the director, passed him, went down to the pew in front and then it stopped, fixed firmly on the lovely Mrs Gaghin Farrit.

His voice rose. '*I arrest you for the crime of harassment and unlawful and threatening behaviour to a Church of Scotland minister.*'

Farrit screamed and made a dive for the exit, scattering men and women before her.

'Quick, Poalis, grab her!' shouted Sergeant.

Poalis ran to try and head her off but got caught up in the mix-up of scattered bodies. Farrit was almost out the door when the roof fell in on her. Or to put it another way, the contestant for the World's Strongest Lollipop Lady flattened her, and with one beautifully timed combination straight left and right hook, the lovely Mrs Farrit slowly lost consciousness. She also lost her stunning blonde wig, to reveal a bald head.

Sergeant approached me with an endorsement of relief etched in every line of his broadly grinning face.

'I thought you said it was a man?' was all I could think to say.

'I did – she is,' was his not very helpful reply. 'I have to tie up the formalities here,' he said, placing a friendly hand round my shoulder. 'Why don't you and Ephesia go back to the manse for a well-earned cup of tea – or maybe even something a wee bit stronger? I'll be round later to explain everything.'

As we left the church everyone congratulated me, saying it was the best day out in a church they'd ever had. Everyone expressed their admiration for my courage and Ephesia's physical prowess. Indeed, most of the older men couldn't make up their minds as to when they'd seen a better punch. Comparisons between Ephesia and various pugilists were flying thick and fast. One said she could go the distance with Muhammad Ali, another compared her to Rocky Marciano and his trademark Suzie Q punch. But most agreed that physically she was up there with Jersey Joe Wallcot.

R. Sinparsley offered me free haircuts for a year, but I had to promise not to nick his newspapers. I accepted, but only if he in turn would promise not to nick my neck – with his scissors. We left it with negotiations still on-going, as they say in the world of politics.

Old Mr Crabbit also informed us that if ever we needed someone to count the grass on our lawn, he wanted first refusal. I replied that if ever I were going to refuse anyone anything, he would be the first.

So it went on. We were everyone's favourites and they all wished it was next Sunday so they could attend once more. The most used phrase was, 'The telly's rotten on a Sunday anyway.'

I MUST SAY I was relieved to get back to the manse and a generous measure of dry sherry to steady our nerves. Ephesia and I had just steadied our nerves for the fourth time when the front doorbell signalled the arrival of Detective Inspector Sergeant. He was accompanied by the ubiquitous Constable Poalis.

Once we were all seated, Ephesia and I decided our nerves could do with one more steadying in anticipation of Sergeant's summing up as to how he had planned the capture and arrest of my stalker. Sergeant asked our permission to light up his pipe, which we both readily agreed to.

After sucking at it to get it going properly, he took in a mouthful, let it invade the cavities of his mouth and, with a great sigh, blew out the blue aromatic haze into the air.

'Lovely,' he said. As the aroma pervaded the room, Sergeant stared thoughtfully at the fireplace, as if trying to gather his thoughts for the answers to our questions. This was a man who knew how to hold the moment. Finally, he smiled and began to speak.

'Any questions?' was his opening gambit.

I, of course, was awash with them, but the most important one was, 'What made you suspect Mrs Farrit?'

'The obvious ones are always the best, eh!' He sucked in on his pipe again then rose up from the chair and walked towards the living-room window, the one that looked on to Mrs Farrit's house across the street.

'If you remember, when the cat episode was being investigated we interviewed Mrs Farrit and were told that a clown figure on a bicycle had been seen delivering the notes that were put under the windscreen wipers. We presumed that the only way the clown had managed to vanish from the scene was by means of a van that was positioned round the corner out of view from the street residents, and also from any witnesses that would have reacted to him when he left the street and hit the main road. There was only one problem with that assumption. If you remember, that day there was a fall of rain – not heavy, but enough to dampen everything. When I went round the corner to ask if anyone there had seen a van, they said no. I wondered why. I also wondered why there was no dry patch on the street, which there would have been if a van had been parked. No dry patch – so no van. The problem was now, how did someone in full clown make-up manage to virtually disappear?

'I decided to revisit the scene of the crime and I saw that, where your street takes a bend round the corner, there is a lane – a private lane – that leads round the back to Mrs Farrit's backyard, away from prying eyes. A perfect place to vanish in. This was intriguing, but hardly concrete evidence. After all, I had already established through the voice digitaliser that we were dealing with a male, and Mrs Farrit was unlike any male I'd ever met.

'However, the whole thing began to take on an entirely different perspective when you gave me your journal to inspect. Do you remember little Bobby Tarif?'

I thought for a second or so before exclaiming, 'Yes, of course. He used to wear a dress. The boys all used to laugh at me because I dressed like a minister even at that age, but even I used to laugh at wee Bobby. I mean, for goodness sake – a dress. We used to tease him mercilessly.'

Sergeant nodded, then continued speaking. 'You said in your journal that you often wondered what had happened to wee Bobby. I decided to do a little bit of research and to answer your question, he ran away from home and school and was posted as missing.'

'That's right, so he did. I meant what happened after that, though.'

'Well, that was a bit trickier, but eventually I found out that he decided to do what came naturally for a living, and he became a female impersonator. He became a very good one – so good that he drifted into acting and earned a pile of money for a hit production about Jack the Ripper in which he played Jack and *all* of the Ripper victims. A real *tour de force*, for which he was rightly praised.

'However, there was one blot on this otherwise happy ending. The earlier teasing he had endured as a lad had left him very tortured inside and with an enormous inferiority complex. Indeed, he disclosed to us down at the station that, although all of the other children treated him harshly, he'd thought that he could turn to you because you obviously wanted to be a minister – a man of understanding and forgiveness. You were also teased because of the way you dressed, so he very much wanted to befriend you. He thought you were someone who would not let him down.

'But you did, and subsequently he was also pilloried by members of the clergy because of what he did for a living. So he developed a hatred for those who hated him. This grew into a passion as he performed his roles in the Ripper play. And gradually he swapped the image of the women of the night for the men of the cloth. He decided as you had been in at the start of his persecution – a persecution, by the way, that was so bad that he had to run away from it while still a minor – that he would make you pay for his torment by tormenting you.

'This, of course, explained why the voice digitaliser registered as male, because Mrs Farrit was just that. The final clue was one that he left himself. When he phoned you, he used his skill as an actor to disguise his accent – just as he disguised it as Mrs Farrit when we interviewed her – or him. He could not resist leaving a deliberate clue, much the same as the original Jack the Ripper did. If you remember, Reverend, he signed off by saying, "Boye, boye, tara fit now". Of course, when he said it in a Somerset accent it sounded like, "Bye bye, ta ta for now". But when I re-read the transcript I realised that the first six letters of "tara fit now" was "Taraf", and "Boye, boye" said quickly would sound as "Bobby". He had actually given us his name – Bobby Tarif.'

He dragged on his pipe slowly then, staring into the fireplace, said with a touch of melancholy in his voice that added an air of poignancy to the tobacco haze as it drifted round the room, 'You know, there is a part of me that thinks he wanted to be caught. Oh, by the way, there's no such person as Niven Simmons, or Wilson Simmons, or Simpson Simmons. They're all aliases. I checked up the address on the letters from the Synod. Indeed, there is no Synod. Totally fictitious – merely an accommodation address. You were the target of wee Bobby Tarif before you even knew it. Yes, that's right,' he said, anticipating my question. 'When I checked up, the only one seen going in and out of the address was a very attractive blonde lady.'

I could not believe my ears. 'Just a minute, are you saying that the Church of Scotland never gave me an ultimatum, that I am not in danger of being an ex-stipend receiver, and that I can continue to serve as a Church of Scotland minister of the cloth?'

Sergeants' eyes twinkled, signalling this was indeed the case.

'Thank you! Oh, thank you! Can I get you a dry sherry, anything? Have another puff at your pipe. Oh joy! Thank you again. I also forgot to thank you for all the kind things you said about me from the pulpit. I had no idea you thought I was so brave.'

Sergeant exchanged a glance with Poalis. 'Aye well, I only said all of that to wind up our chief suspect. You see, he felt he was now king of the castle and you were a snivelling serf. I wanted to knock that on the head by reversing your positions. I did it so I could observe his reactions and be absolutely sure I had the right man.'

Ephesia's voice boomed over the room, 'I don't know about

you, Inspector, but I'm sure *I* have the right man and I know that he has the right woman.'

I could see the sherry was having its effect on Ephesia. I saw Sergeant nod to Poalis to make their exit and I heard Poalis say as they left the room, 'We'll thee how brave he ith now.'

I think I heard them both laugh, then Ephesia was upon me and, as someone once said, 'The rest is silence.'

Postscript

I HAVE DECIDED to put pen to paper one last time, solely to record a happening that has once again turned my world on its head and left me reeling with the possible consequences.

I was settling down this morning to read the extensive coverage in the newspapers of my wee adventure. They had been reporting it for the last week in serial form, and I must say I had come out of it rather well – indeed, there has been talk of turning it into a film.

The representative of the film company asked me who I thought should portray me. Modestly, I suggested Clarke Gable. Unfortunately, he's dead, apparently, so I offered an alternative of Cary Grant – again deceased. Spencer Tracy? The same. I felt very sad that all these wonderful stars have missed out on the opportunity to add one last Oscar to their collection. The film company have suggested someone called Bruce Willis. I said I'd never heard of him, still if it helped him to get started in his career I'm delighted for him.

The film representative then asked who would play Ephesia. Ephesia suggested a Cameron Diaz? I suggested a Cameron Highlander. Ephesia went into Muhammad Ali mode. I went into hiding. Eventually, she gave up looking for me and left the manse with the film representative to scout for locations.

As I said, I was reading the newspapers when the doorbell rang. Keeking through the curtain I could see that it was a clergyman at the door. Intrigued, I walked through the hall and opened it to reveal a rather small, middle-aged gentleman who introduced himself as the Very Reverend Ewan Mee. He asked if I could grant him fifteen minutes of my time. As Ephesia would not be back seeking revenge for at least an hour, I bade him to enter.

As he sat down, he glanced quickly round the room, shook his head and began to speak.

'Reverend Jolly,' he began in a voice that tried desperately to avoid using the vowel 'a'. 'Eh hev been esked to inform you thet you hev been selected to ect es Her Mejesty's Cheplain et Belmorel Cestle.'

'E don't – I mean, I don't understand. Why me?'

'It's enterily understendeble thet you're perplexed,' he went on. 'Ellow me to explain. Every year the Church sends Her Mejesty a wee pressy to celebrate Christmes. Just a wee token, you understend. Well, this year we sent a wee letter to esk her if we could send her holly. Unfortunately, the men who typed out the letter hed a wee bit of a mistake in the missive. You may not be ewair, but on the typewriter keyboard the letter 'h' is right next to the letter 'j', so it is. End lo end behold, did he not wind up esking Her Mejesty could we send her *Jolly* for Christmes?

'We were in the throes of informing Her Mejesty of our wee mistake, when eh letter errived with the Royel Seal which sed, "Her Mejesty hes read in the newspapers of the exploits of The Reverend Jolly end is ebsolutely thrilled thet he is to be her Cheplain, as the Royal Pelis could do with a cherecter such es him to keep things lively."

'So Eh'm here to tell you thet you're off to Belmorel et the end of the month. Of course, your selery will hev to rezz eccordingly.

'It's been lovely talking et you. Eh'll see meself out. Thenks egain.'

And he was off.

As I sat dumbfoonered in my favourite old chair, my mind

went over the events that had led me to write this journal. From seemingly being threatened with everything from eviction to extinction, I was now in a position I could only have dreamed of. At times, I thought the Lord had deserted me. Now I know he had only been testing me. He hadn't left, He had merely hidden, and I had to find him.

I smiled as I wondered how many other times He had played hide and seek with the human race.